Designing Machine Learning Systems with Python

Design efficient machine learning systems that give you more accurate results

David Julian

[PACKT] open source *
PUBLISHING   community experience distilled

BIRMINGHAM - MUMBAI

Designing Machine Learning Systems with Python

First published: April 2016

Production reference: 1310316

Published by Packt Publishing Ltd.
Livery Place
35 Livery Street
Birmingham B3 2PB, UK.

ISBN 978-1-78588-295-1

www.packtpub.com

Credits

Author
David Julian

Reviewer
Dr. Vahid Mirjalili

Commissioning Editor
Veena Pagare

Acquisition Editor
Tushar Gupta

Content Development Editor
Merint Thomas Mathew

Technical Editor
Abhishek R. Kotian

Copy Editor
Angad Singh

Project Coordinator
Suzanne Coutinho

Proofreader
Safis Editing

Indexer
Rekha Nair

Graphics
Disha Haria

Jason Monteiro

Production Coordinator
Aparna Bhagat

Cover Work
Aparna Bhagat

About the Author

David Julian is currently working on a machine learning project with Urban Ecological Systems Ltd and Blue Smart Farms (`http://www.bluesmartfarms.com.au`) to detect and predict insect infestation in greenhouse crops. He is currently collecting a labeled training set that includes images and environmental data (temperature, humidity, soil moisture, and pH), linking this data to observations of infestation (the target variable), and using it to train neural net models. The aim is to create a model that will reduce the need for direct observation, be able to anticipate insect outbreaks, and subsequently control conditions. There is a brief outline of the project at `http://davejulian.net/projects/ues`. David also works as a data analyst, I.T. consultant, and trainer.

I would like to thank Hogan Gleeson, James Fuller, Kali McLaughlin and Nadine Miller. This book would not have been possible without the great work of the open source machine learning community.

About the Reviewer

Dr. Vahid Mirjalili is a data scientist with a diverse background in engineering, mathematics, and computer science. With his specialty in data mining, he is very interested in predictive modeling and getting insights from data. Currently, he is working towards publishing a book on big data analysis, which covers a wide range of tools and techniques for analyzing massive data sets. Furthermore, as a Python developer, he likes to contribute to the open source community. He has developed Python packages for data clustering, such as PyClust. A collection of his tutorials and programs on data science can be found in his Github repository at `http://github.com/mirjalil/DataScience`. For more information, please visit his personal website at `http://vahidmirjalili.com`.

www.PacktPub.com

eBooks, discount offers, and more

Did you know that Packt offers eBook versions of every book published, with PDF and ePub files available? You can upgrade to the eBook version at www.PacktPub.com and as a print book customer, you are entitled to a discount on the eBook copy. Get in touch with us at customercare@packtpub.com for more details.

At www.PacktPub.com, you can also read a collection of free technical articles, sign up for a range of free newsletters and receive exclusive discounts and offers on Packt books and eBooks.

https://www2.packtpub.com/books/subscription/packtlib

Do you need instant solutions to your IT questions? PacktLib is Packt's online digital book library. Here, you can search, access, and read Packt's entire library of books.

Why subscribe?

- Fully searchable across every book published by Packt
- Copy and paste, print, and bookmark content
- On demand and accessible via a web browser

Table of Contents

Preface

Machine learning is one of the biggest trends that the world of computing has seen. Machine learning systems have a profound and exciting ability to provide important insights on an amazing variety of applications, from ground-breaking and lifesaving medical research to discovering fundamental physical aspects of our universe; from providing us with better, cleaner food to web analytics and economic modeling. In fact, there is hardly any area of our lives that is not touched by this technology in some way. Everyone wants to get into the field of machine learning, and in order to obtain sufficient recognition in this field, one must be able to understand and design a machine learning system that serves the needs of a project.

What this book covers

Chapter 1, *Thinking in Machine Learning*, gets you started with the basics of machine learning, and as the title says, it will help you think in the machine learning paradigm. You will learn the design principles and various models involved in machine learning.

Chapter 2, *Tools and Techniques*, explains that Python comes equipped with a large library of packages for machine learning tasks. This chapter will give you a flavor of some huge libraries. It will cover packages such as NumPy, SciPy, Matplotlib, and Scilit-learn.

Chapter 3, *Turning Data into Information*, explains that raw data can be in many different formats and can be of varying quantity and quality. Sometimes, we are overwhelmed by data, and sometimes we struggle to get every last drop of information from our data. For data to become information, it requires some meaningful structure. In this chapter, we will introduce some broad topics such as big data, data properties, data sources, and data processing and analysis.

Chapter 4, *Models – Learning from Information*, takes you through the logical models—where we explore a logical language and create a hypothesis space mapping, tree models – where we will find that they can be applied to a wide range of tasks and are both descriptive and easy to interpret; and rule models – where we discuss both ordered rule list- and unordered rule set-based models.

Chapter 5, *Linear Models*, introduces one of the most widely used models that forms the foundation of many advanced nonlinear techniques, such as support vector machines and neural networks. In this chapter, we will study some of the most commonly used techniques in machine learning. We will create hypothesis representations for linear and logistic regression.

Chapter 6, *Neural Networks*, introduces the powerful machine learning algorithm of artificial neural networks. We will see how these networks are a simplified model of neurons in the brain.

Chapter 7, *Features – How Algorithms See the World*, goes through the different types of feature—the Quantitative, Ordinal, and Categorical features. We will also learn the Structured and Transforming features in detail.

Chapter 8, *Learning with Ensembles*, explains the reason behind the motivation for creating machine learning ensembles, which comes from clear intuitions and is grounded in a rich theoretical history. The types of machine learning ensemble that can be created are as diverse as the models themselves, and the main considerations revolve around three things: how we divide our data, how we select the models, and the methods we use to combine their results.

Chapter 9, *Design Strategies and Case Studies*, looks at some design strategies to ensure your machine learning applications perform optimally. We will learn model selection and parameter tuning techniques, and apply them to several case studies.

What you need for this book

All you need is an inclination to learn machine learning and the Python V3 software, which you can download from `https://www.python.org/downloads/`.

Who this book is for

This book is for data scientists, scientists, or just the curious. You will need to know some linear algebra and some Python. You will need to have some basic knowledge of machine learning concepts.

Conventions

In this book, you will find a number of text styles that distinguish between different kinds of information. Here are some examples of these styles and an explanation of their meaning.

Code words in text, database table names, folder names, filenames, file extensions, pathnames, dummy URLs, user input, and Twitter handles are shown as follows: "NumPy uses a `dtype` object to describe various aspects of the data."

Any command-line input or output is written as follows:

```
import numpy as np
import matplotlib.pyplot as plt

x = np.arange(0., 5., 0.2)
plt.plot(x, x**4, 'r', x, x*90, 'bs', x, x**3, 'g^')
plt.show()
```

New terms and **important words** are shown in bold. Words that you see on the screen, for example, in menus or dialog boxes, appear in the text like this: "Clicking the **Next** button moves you to the next screen."

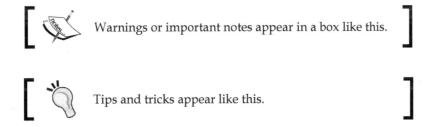

Warnings or important notes appear in a box like this.

Tips and tricks appear like this.

Reader feedback

Feedback from our readers is always welcome. Let us know what you think about this book—what you liked or disliked. Reader feedback is important for us as it helps us develop titles that you will really get the most out of.

To send us general feedback, simply e-mail `feedback@packtpub.com`, and mention the book's title in the subject of your message.

If there is a topic that you have expertise in and you are interested in either writing or contributing to a book, see our author guide at `www.packtpub.com/authors`.

Customer support

Now that you are the proud owner of a Packt book, we have a number of things to help you to get the most from your purchase.

Downloading the example code

You can download the example code files for this book from your account at http://www.packtpub.com. If you purchased this book elsewhere, you can visit http://www.packtpub.com/support and register to have the files e-mailed directly to you.

You can download the code files by following these steps:

1. Log in or register to our website using your e-mail address and password.
2. Hover the mouse pointer on the **SUPPORT** tab at the top.
3. Click on **Code Downloads & Errata**.
4. Enter the name of the book in the **Search** box.
5. Select the book for which you're looking to download the code files.
6. Choose from the drop-down menu where you purchased this book from.
7. Click on **Code Download**.

Once the file is downloaded, please make sure that you unzip or extract the folder using the latest version of:

* WinRAR / 7-Zip for Windows
* Zipeg / iZip / UnRarX for Mac
* 7-Zip / PeaZip for Linux

Errata

Although we have taken every care to ensure the accuracy of our content, mistakes do happen. If you find a mistake in one of our books—maybe a mistake in the text or the code—we would be grateful if you could report this to us. By doing so, you can save other readers from frustration and help us improve subsequent versions of this book. If you find any errata, please report them by visiting http://www.packtpub.com/submit-errata, selecting your book, clicking on the **Errata Submission Form** link, and entering the details of your errata. Once your errata are verified, your submission will be accepted and the errata will be uploaded to our website or added to any list of existing errata under the Errata section of that title.

To view the previously submitted errata, go to https://www.packtpub.com/books/content/support and enter the name of the book in the search field. The required information will appear under the **Errata** section.

Piracy

Piracy of copyrighted material on the Internet is an ongoing problem across all media. At Packt, we take the protection of our copyright and licenses very seriously. If you come across any illegal copies of our works in any form on the Internet, please provide us with the location address or website name immediately so that we can pursue a remedy.

Please contact us at copyright@packtpub.com with a link to the suspected pirated material.

We appreciate your help in protecting our authors and our ability to bring you valuable content.

Questions

If you have a problem with any aspect of this book, you can contact us at questions@packtpub.com, and we will do our best to address the problem.

1
Thinking in Machine Learning

Machine learning systems have a profound and exciting ability to provide important insights to an amazing variety of applications; from groundbreaking and life-saving medical research, to discovering fundamental physical aspects of our universe. From providing us with better, cleaner food, to web analytics and economic modeling. In fact, there are hardly any areas of our lives that have not been touched by this technology in some way. With an expanding Internet of Things, there is a staggering amount of data being generated, and it is clear that intelligent systems are changing societies in quite dramatic ways. With open source tools, such those provided by Python and its libraries, and the increasing open source knowledge base represented by the Web, it is relatively easy and cheap to learn and apply this technology in new and exciting ways. In this chapter, we will cover the following topics:

- Human interface
- Design principles
- Models
- Unified modelling language

The human interface

For those of you old enough, or unfortunate enough, to have used early versions of the Microsoft office suite, you will probably remember the Mr Clippy office assistant. This feature, first introduced in Office 97, popped up uninvited from the bottom right-hand side of your computer screen every time you typed the word 'Dear' at the beginning of a document, with the prompt "it looks like you are writing a letter, would you like help with that?".

Mr Clippy, turned on by default in early versions of Office, was almost universally derided by users of the software and could go down in history as one of machine learning's first big fails.

So, why was the cheery Mr Clippy so hated? Clearly the folks at Microsoft, at the forefront of consumer software development, were not stupid, and the idea that an automated assistant could help with day to day office tasks is not necessarily a bad idea. Indeed, later incarnations of automated assistants, the best ones at least, operate seamlessly in the background and provide a demonstrable increase in work efficiency. Consider predictive text. There are many examples, some very funny, of where predictive text has gone spectacularly wrong, but in the majority of cases where it doesn't fail, it goes unnoticed. It just becomes part of our normal work flow.

At this point, we need a distinction between error and failure. Mr Clippy failed because it was obtrusive and poorly designed, not necessarily because it was in error; that is, it could make the right suggestion, but chances are you already know that you are writing a letter. Predictive text has a high error rate, that is, it often gets the prediction wrong, but it does not fail largely because of the way it is designed to fail: unobtrusively.

The design of any system that has a *tightly coupled human interface*, to use systems engineering speak, is difficult. Human behavior, like the natural world in general, is not something we can always predict. Expression recognition systems, natural language processing, and gesture recognition technology, amongst other things, all open up new ways of human-machine interaction, and this has important applications for the machine learning specialist.

Whenever we are designing a system that requires human input, we need to anticipate the possible ways, not just the intended ways, a human will interact with the system. In essence, what we are trying to do with these systems is to instil in them some understanding of the broad panorama of human experience.

In the first years of the web, search engines used a simple system based on the number of times search terms appeared in articles. Web developers soon began gaming the system by increasing the number of key search terms. Clearly, this would lead to a keyword arms race and result in a very boring web. The page rank system measuring the number of quality inbound links was designed to provide a more accurate search result. Now, of course, modern search engines use more sophisticated and secret algorithms.

What is also important for ML designers is the ever increasing amount of data that is being generated. This presents several challenges, most notably its sheer vastness. However, the power of algorithms in extracting knowledge and insights that would not have been possible with smaller data sets is massive. So, many human interactions are now digitized, and we are only just beginning to understand and explore the many ways in which this data can be used.

As a curious example, consider the study *The expression of emotion in 20th century books* (Acerbi et al, 2013). Though strictly more of a data analysis study, rather than machine learning, it is illustrative for several reasons. Its purpose was to chart the emotional content, in terms of a mood score, of text extracted from books of the 20th century. With access to a large volume of digitized text through the project Gutenberg digital library, WordNet (`http://wordnet.princeton.edu/wordnet/`), and Google's **Ngram** database (`books.google.com/ngrams`), the authors of this study were able to map cultural change over the 20th century as reflected in the literature of the time. They did this by mapping trends in the usage of the *mood* words.

For this study, the authors labeled each word (*a 1gram*) and associated it with a mood score and the year it was published. We can see that emotion words, such as joy, sadness, fear, and so forth, can be scored according to the positive or negative mood they evoke. The mood score was obtained from WordNet (`wordnet.princeton.edu`). WordNet assigns an affect score to each mood word. Finally, the authors simply counted the occurrences of each mood word:

$$M = \frac{1}{n}\sum_{i=1}^{n}\frac{c_i}{C_{the}} \quad M_z = \frac{M - \mu_M}{\sigma_M}$$

Here, ci is the count of a particular mood word, n is the total count of mood words (not all words, just words with a mood score), and C_{the} is the count of the word *the* in the text. This normalizes the sum to take into account that some years more books were written (or digitized). Also, since many later books tend to contain more technical language, the word *the* was used to normalize rather than get the total word count. This gives a more accurate representation of emotion over a long time period in prose text. Finally, the score is normalized according to a normal distribution, M_z, by subtracting the mean and dividing by the standard deviation.

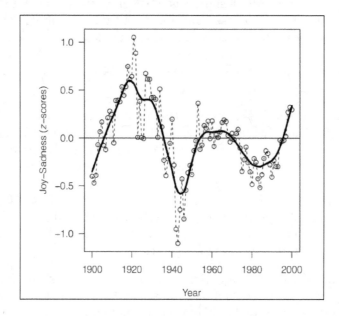

This figure is taken from *The expression of Emotions in 20th Century Books, (Alberto Acerbi, Vasileios Lampos, Phillip Garnett, R. Alexander Bentley) PLOS*.

Here we can see one of the graphs generated by this study. It shows the joy-sadness score for books written in this period, and clearly shows a negative trend associated with the period of World War II.

This study is interesting for several reasons. Firstly, it is an example of data-driven science, where previously considered *soft* sciences, such as sociology and anthropology, are given a solid empirical footing. Despite some pretty impressive results, this study was relatively easy to implement. This is mainly because most of the hard work had already been done by WordNet and Google. This highlights how using data resources that are freely available on the Internet, and software tools such as the Python's data and machine learning packages, anyone with the data skills and motivation can build on this work.

Design principles

An analogy is often made between systems design and designing other things such as a house. To a certain extent, this analogy holds true. We are attempting to place design components into a structure that meets a specification. The analogy breaks down when we consider their respective operating environments. It is generally assumed in the design of a house that the landscape, once suitably formed, will not change.

Software environments are slightly different. Systems are interactive and dynamic. Any system that we design will be nested inside other systems, either electronic, physical, or human. In the same way different layers in computer networks (application layer, transport layer, physical layer, and so on) nest different sets of meanings and function, so to do activities performed at different levels of a project.

As the designer of these systems, we must also have a strong awareness of the setting, that is, the domain in which we work. This knowledge gives us clues to patterns in our data and helps us give context to our work.

Machine learning projects can be divided into five distinct activities, shown as follows:

- Defining the object and specification
- Preparing and exploring the data
- Model building
- Implementation
- Testing
- Deployment

The designer is mainly concerned with the first three. However, they often play, and in many projects must play, a major role in other activities. It should also be said that a project's timeline is not necessarily a linear sequence of these activities. The important point is that they are distinct activities. They may occur in parallel to each other, and in other ways interact with each other, but they generally involve different types of tasks that can be separated in terms of human and other resources, the stage of the project, and externalities. Also, we need to consider that different activities involve distinct operational modes. Consider the different ways in which your brain works when you are sketching out an idea, as compared to when you are working on a specific analytical task, say a piece of code.

Often, the hardest question is where to begin. We can start drilling into the different elements of a problem, with an idea of a feature set and perhaps an idea of the model or models we might use. This may lead to a defined object and specification, or we may have to do some preliminary research such as checking possible data sets and sources, available technologies, or talking to other engineers, technicians, and users of the system. We need to explore the operating environment and the various constraints; is it part of a web application, or is it a laboratory research tool for scientists?

In the early stages of design, our work flow will flip between working on the different elements. For instance, we start with a general problem—perhaps having an idea of the task, or tasks, necessary to solve it—then we divide it into what we think are the key features, try it out on a few models with a toy dataset, go back to refine the feature set, adjust our model, precisely define tasks, and refine the model. When we feel our system is robust enough, we can test it out on some real data. Of course, then we may need to go back and change our feature set.

Selecting and optimizing features is often a major activity (really, a task in itself) for the machine learning designer. We cannot really decide what features we need until we have adequately described the task, and of course, both the task and features are constrained by the types of feasible models we can build.

Types of questions

As designers, we are asked to solve a problem. We are given some data and an expected output. The first step is to frame the problem in a way that a machine can understand it, and in a way that carries meaning for a human. The following six broad approaches are what we can take to precisely define our machine learning problem:

- **Exploratory**: Here, we analyze data, looking for patterns such as a trend or relationship between variables. Exploration will often lead to a hypothesis such as linking diet with disease, or crime rate with urban dwellings.

- **Descriptive**: Here, we try to summarize specific features of our data. For instance, the average life expectancy, average temperature, or the number of left-handed people in a population.

- **Inferential**: An inferential question is one that attempts to support a hypothesis, for instance, proving (or disproving) a general link between life expectancy and income by using different data sets.

- **Predictive**: Here, we are trying to anticipate future behavior. For instance, predicting life expectancy by analyzing income.

- **Casual**: This is an attempt to find out what causes something. Does low income cause a lower life expectancy?
- **Mechanistic**: This tries to answer questions such as "what are the mechanisms that link income with life expectancy?"

Most machine learning problems involve several of these types of questions during development. For instance, we may first explore the data looking for patterns or trends, and then we may describe certain key features of our data. This may enable us to make a prediction, and find a cause or a mechanism behind a particular problem.

Are you asking the right question?

The question must be plausible and meaningful in its subject area. This domain knowledge enables you to understand the things that are important in your data and to see where a certain pattern or correlation has meaning.

The question should be as specific as possible, while still giving a meaningful answer. It is common for it to begin as a generalized statement, such as "I wonder if wealthy means healthy". So, you do some further research and find you can get statistics for wealth by geographic region, say from the tax office. We can measure health through its inverse, that is, illness, say by hospital admissions, and we can test our initial proposition, "wealthy means healthy", by tying illness to geographic region. We can see that a more specific question relies on several, perhaps questionable, assumptions.

We should also consider that our results may be confounded by the fact that poorer people may not have healthcare insurance, so are less likely to go to a hospital despite illness. There is an interaction between what we want to find out and what we are trying to measure. This interaction perhaps hides a true rate of illness. All is not lost, however. Because we know about these things, then perhaps we can account for them in our model.

We can make things a lot easier by learning as much as we can about the domain we are working in.

You could possibly save yourself a lot of time by checking whether the question you are asking, or part of it, has already been answered, or if there are data sets available that may shed some light on that topic. Often, you have to approach a problem from several different angles at once. Do as much preparatory research as you can. It is quite likely that other designers have done work that could shed light on your own.

Tasks

A task is a specific activity conducted over a period of time. We have to distinguish between the human tasks (planning, designing, and implementing) to the machine tasks (classification, clustering, regression, and so on). Also consider when there is overlap between human and machine, for example, as in selecting features for a model. Our true goal in machine learning is to transform as many of these tasks as we can from human tasks to machine tasks.

It is not always easy to match a real world problem to a specific task. Many real world problems may seem to be conceptually linked but require a very different solution. Alternatively, problems that appear completely different may require similar methods. Unfortunately, there is no simple lookup table to match a particular task to a problem. A lot depends on the setting and domain. A similar problem in one domain may be unsolvable in another, perhaps because of lack of data. There are, however, a small number of tasks that are applied to a large number of methods to solve many of the most common problem types. In other words, in the space of all possible programming tasks, there is a subset of tasks that are useful to our particular problem. Within this subset, there is a smaller subset of tasks that are easy and can actually be applied usefully to our problem.

Machine learning tasks occur in three broad settings:

- **Supervised learning**: The goal here is to learn a model from labeled training data that allows predictions to be made on unseen future data.

- **Unsupervised learning**: Here we deal with unlabeled data and our goal is to find hidden patterns in this data to extract meaningful information.

- **Reinforcement learning**: The goal here is to develop a system that improves its performance based on the interactions it has with its environment. This usually involves a reward signal. This is similar to supervised learning, except that rather than having a labeled training set, reinforcement learning uses a reward function to continually improve its performance.

Now, let's take a look at some of the major machine learning tasks. The following diagram should give you a starting point to try and decide what type of task is appropriate for different machine learning problems:

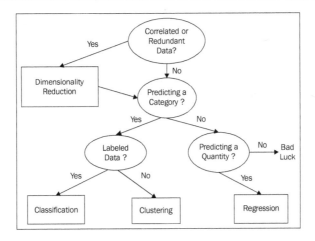

Classification

Classification is probably the most common type of task; this is due in part to the fact that it is relatively easy, well understood, and solves a lot of common problems. Classification is about assigning classes to a set of instances, based on their features. This is a supervised learning method because it relies on a labeled training set to learn a set of model parameters. This model can then be applied to unlabeled data to make a prediction on what class each instance belongs to. There are broadly two types of classification tasks: **binary classification** and **multiclass classification**. A typical binary classification task is e-mail spam detection. Here we use the contents of an e-mail to determine if it belongs to one of the two classes: spam or not spam. An example of multiclass classification is handwriting recognition, where we try to predict a class, for example, the letter name. In this case, we have one class for each of the alpha numeric characters. Multiclass classification can sometimes be achieved by chaining binary classification tasks together, however, we lose information this way, and we are unable to define a single decision boundary. For this reason, multiclass classification is often treated separately from binary classification.

Regression

There are cases where what we are interested in are not discrete classes, but a continuous variable, for instance, a probability. These types of problems are regression problems. The aim of regression analysis is to understand how changes to the input, independent variables, effect changes to the dependent variable. The simplest regression problems are linear and involve fitting a straight line to a set of data in order to make a prediction. This is usually done by minimizing the sum of squared errors in each instance in the training set. Typical regression problems include estimating the likelihood of a disease given a range and severity of symptoms, or predicting test scores given past performance.

Clustering

Clustering is the most well known unsupervised method. Here, we are concerned with making a measurement of similarity between instances in an unlabeled dataset. We often use geometric models to determine the distance between instances, based on their feature values. We can use an arbitrary measurement of closeness to determine what cluster each instance belongs to. Clustering is often used in data mining and exploratory data analysis. There are a large variety of methods and algorithms that perform this task, and some of the approaches include the distance-based method, as well as finding a center point for each cluster, or using statistical techniques based on distributions.

Related to clustering is association; this is an unsupervised task to find a certain type of pattern in the data. This task is behind product recommender systems such as those provided by Amazon and other on-line shops.

Dimensionality reduction

Many data sets contain a large number of features or measurements associated with each instance. This can present a challenge in terms of computational power and memory allocation. Also many features may contain redundant information or information that is correlated to other features. In these cases, the performance of our learning model may be significantly degraded. Dimensionality reduction is most often used in feature prepossessing; it compresses the data into a lower dimension sub space while retaining useful information. Dimensionality reduction is also used when we want to visualize data, typically by projecting higher dimensions onto one, two, or three dimensions.

From these basic machine tasks, there are a number of derived tasks. In many applications, this may simply be applying the learning model to a prediction to establish a casual relationship. We must remember that explaining and predicting are not the same. A model can make a prediction, but unless we know explicitly how it made the prediction, we cannot begin to form a comprehensible explanation. An explanation requires human knowledge of the domain.

We can also use a prediction model to find exceptions from a general pattern. Here we are interested in the individual cases that deviate from the predictions. This is often called **anomaly detection** and has wide applications in things like detecting bank fraud, noise filtering, and even in the search for extraterrestrial life.

An important and potentially useful task is subgroup discovery. Our goal here is not, as in clustering, to partition the entire domain, but rather to find a subgroup that has a substantially different distribution. In essence, subgroup discovery is trying to find relationships between a dependent target variables and many independent explaining variables. We are not trying to find a complete relationship, but rather a group of instances that are different in ways that are important to the domain. For instance, establishing a subgroup, *smoker = true* and *family history = true* for a target variable of *heart disease = true*.

Finally, we consider control type tasks. These act to optimize control settings to maximize a payoff, given different conditions. This can be achieved in several ways. We can clone expert behavior: the machine learns directly from a human and makes predictions on actions given different conditions. The task is to learn a prediction model for the expert's actions. This is similar to reinforcement learning, where the task is to learn a relationship between conditions and optimal action.

Errors

In machine learning systems, software flaws can have very serious real world consequences; what happens if your algorithm, embedded in an assembly line robot, classifies a human as a production component? Clearly, in critical systems, you need to plan for failure. There should be a robust fault and error detection procedure embedded in your design process and systems.

Sometimes it is necessary to design very complex systems simply for the purpose of debugging and checking for logic flaws. It may be necessary to generate data sets with specific statistical structures, or create *artificial humans* to mimic an interface. For example, developing a methodology to verify that the logic of your design is sound at the data, model, and task levels. Errors can be hard to track, and as a scientist, you must assume that there are errors and try to prove otherwise.

The idea of recognizing and gracefully catching errors is important for the software designer, but as machine learning systems designers, we must take it a step further. We need to be able to capture, in our models, the ability to learn from an error.

Consideration must be given to how we select our test set, and in particular, how representative it is of the rest of the dataset. For instance, if it is noisy compared to the training set, it will give poor results on the test set, suggesting that our model is overfitting, when in fact, this is not the case. To avoid this, a process of cross validation is used. This works by randomly dividing the data into, for example, ten chunks of equal size. We use nine chunks for training the model and one for testing. We do this 10 times, using each chunk once for testing. Finally, we take an average of test set performance. Cross validation is used with other supervised learning problems besides classification, but as you would expect, unsupervised learning problems need to be evaluated differently.

With an unsupervised task we do not have a labeled training set. Evaluation can therefore be a little tricky since we do not know what a correct answer looks like. In a clustering problem, for instance, we can compare the quality of different models by measures such as the ratio of cluster diameter compared to the distance between clusters. However, in problems of any complexity, we can never tell if there is another model, not yet built, which is better.

Optimization

Optimization problems are ubiquitous in many different domains, such as finance, business, management, sciences, mathematics, and engineering. Optimization problems consist of the following:

- An objective function that we want to maximize or minimize.

- Decision variables, that is, a set of controllable inputs. These inputs are varied within the specified constraints in order to satisfy the objective function.

- Parameters, which are uncontrollable or fixed inputs.

- Constraints are relations between decision variables and parameters. They define what values the decision variables can have.

Most optimization problems have a single objective function. In the cases where we may have multiple objective functions, we often find that they conflict with each other, for example, reducing costs and increasing output. In practice, we try to reformulate multiple objectives into a single function, perhaps by creating a weighted combination of objective functions. In our costs and output example, a variable along the lines of cost per unit might work.

The decision variables are the variables we control to achieve the objective. They may include things such as resources or labor. The parameters of the module are fixed for each run of the model. We may use several *cases*, where we choose different parameters to test variations in multiple conditions.

There are literally thousands of solution algorithms to the many different types of optimization problems. Most of them involve first finding a feasible solution, then iteratively improving on it by adjusting the decision variables to hopefully find an optimum solution. Many optimization problems can be solved reasonably well with linear programming techniques. They assume that the objective function and all the constraints are linear with respect to the decision variables. Where these relationships are not linear, we often use a suitable quadratic function. If the system is non-linear, then the objective function may not be convex. That is, it may have more than one local minima, and there is no assurance that a local minima is a global minima.

Linear programming

Why are linear models so ubiquitous? Firstly, they are relatively easy to understand and implement. They are based on a well founded mathematical theory that was developed around the mid 1700s and that later played a pivotal role in the development of the digital computer. Computers are uniquely tasked to implement linear programs because computers were conceptualized largely on the basis of the theory of linear programming. Linear functions are always convex, meaning they have only one minima. **Linear Programming** (**LP**) problems are usually solved using the simplex method. Suppose that we want to solve the optimization problem, we would use the following syntax:

max $x_1 + x_2$ with constraints: $2x_1 + x_2 \leq 4$ and $x_1 + 2x_2 \leq 3$

We assume that x_1 and x_2 are greater than or equal to 0. The first thing we need to do is convert it to the standard form. This is done by ensuring the problem is a maximization problem, that is, we convert *min z* to *max -z*. We also need to convert the inequalities to equalities by adding non-negative slack variables. The example here is already a maximization problem, so we can leave our objective function as it is. We do need to change the inequalities in the constraints to equalities:

$2x_1 + x_2 + x_3 = 4$ and $x_1 + 2x_2 + x_4 = 3$

If we let *z* denote the value of the objective function, we can then write the following:

$z - x_1 - x_2 = 0$

We now have the following system of linear equations:

- Objective: $z - x_1 - x_2 + 0 + 0 = 0$
- Constraint 1: $2x_1 + x_2 + x_3 + 0 = 4$
- Constraint 2: $x_1 + 2x_2 + 0 + x_4 = 3$

Our objective is to maximize *z*, remembering that all variables are non-negative. We can see that x_1 and x_2 appear in all the equations and are called non-basic. The x_3 and x_4 value only appear in one equation each. They are called basic variables. We can find a basic solution by assigning all non-basic variables to 0. Here, this gives us the following:

$x_1 = x_2 = 0; x_3 = 4; x_4 = 3; z = 0$

Is this an optimum solution, remembering that our goal is to maximize z? We can see that since z subtracts x_1 and x_2 in the first equation in our linear system, we are able to increase these variables. If the coefficients in this equation were all non-negative, then there would be no way to increase z. We will know that we have found an optimum solution when all coefficients in the objective equation are positive.

This is not the case here. So, we take one of the non-basic variables with a negative coefficient in the objective equation (say x_1, which is called the **entering variable**) and use a technique called **pivoting** to turn it from a non-basic to a basic variable. At the same time, we will change a basic variable, called the **leaving variable**, into a non-basic one. We can see that x_1 appears in both the constraint equations, so which one do we choose to pivot? Remembering that we need to keep the coefficients positive. We find that by using the pivot element that yields the lowest ratio of right-hand side of the equations to their respective entering coefficients, we can find another basic solution. For x_1, in this example, it gives us 4/2 for the first constraint and 3/1 for the second. So, we will pivot using x_1 in constraint 1.

We divide constraint 1 by 2, and get the following:

$x_1 + ½ x_2 + ½ x_3 = 2$

We can now write this in terms of x_1, and substitute it into the other equations to eliminate $x1$ from those equations. Once we have performed a bit of algebra, we end up with the following linear system:

$z - 1/2x_2 + 1/3 x_3 = 2$

$x_1 + 1/2 x_2 + 1/2x_3 = 2$

$3/2x_2 - 1/2x_3 + x_4 = 1$

We have another basic solution. But, is this the optimal solution? Since we still have a minus coefficient in the first equation, the answer is no. We can now go through the same pivot process with $x2$, and using the ratio rule, we find that we can pivot on $3/2x2$ in the third equation. This gives us the following:

$z + 1/3x_3 + 1/3x_4 = 7/3$

$x1 + 2/3x_3 - 1/3 x_4 = 5/3$

$x2 - 1/3x_3 + 2/3 x_4 = 2/3$

This gives us the solution to $x_3 = x_4 = 0$, $x_1 = 5/3$, $x2 = 2/3$, and $z = 7/3$. This is the optimal solution because there are no more negatives in the first equation.

We can visualize this with the following graph. The shaded area is the region where we will find a feasible solution:

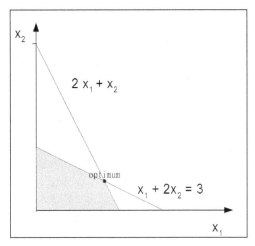

The two variable optimization problem

Models

Linear programming gives us a strategy for encoding real world problems into the language of computers. However, we must remember that our goal is not to just solve an instance of a problem, but to create a model that will solve unique problems from new data. This is the essence of learning. A learning model must have a mechanism to evaluate its output, and in turn, change its behavior to a state that is closer to a solution.

The model is essentially a hypothesis, that is, a proposed explanation of a phenomena. The goal is for it to apply a generalization to the problem. In the case of a supervised learning problem, knowledge gained from the training set is applied to the unlabeled test. In the case of an unsupervised learning problem, such as clustering, the system does not learn from a training set. It must learn from the characteristics of the data set itself, such as the degree of similarity. In both cases, the process is iterative. It repeats a well-defined set of tasks, which moves the model closer to a correct hypothesis.

Models are the core of a machine learning system. They are what does the learning. There are many models, with as many variations on these models, as there are unique solutions. We can see that the problems machine learning systems solve (regression, classification, association, and so on) come up in many different settings. They have been used successfully in almost all branches of science, engineering, mathematics, commerce, and also in the social sciences; they are as diverse as the domains they operate in.

This diversity of models gives machine learning systems great problem solving power. However, it can also be a bit daunting for the designer to decide which is the best model, or models, are for a particular problem. To complicate things, there are often several models that may solve your task, or your task may need several models. Which is the most accurate and efficient pathway through an original problem is something you simply cannot know when you embark upon such a project.

For our purposes here, let's break this broad canvas into three overlapping, non-mutual, and exclusive categories: geometric, probabilistic, and logical. Within these three models, a distinction must be made regarding how a model divides up the instance space. The instance space can be considered as all the possible instances of your data, regardless of whether each instance appears in the data. The actual data is a subset of the space of the instance space.

There are two approaches to dividing up this space: grouping and grading. The key difference between the two is that grouping models divide the instance space into fixed discrete units called **segments**. They have a finite resolution and cannot distinguish between classes beyond this resolution. Grading, on the other hand, forms a global model over the entire instance space, rather than dividing the space into segments. In theory, their resolution is infinite, and they can distinguish between instances no matter how similar they are. The distinction between grouping and grading is not absolute, and many models contain elements of both. For instance, a linear classifier is generally considered a grading model because it is based on a continuous function. However, there are instances that the linear model cannot distinguish between, for example, a line or surface parallel to the decision boundary.

Geometric models

Geometric models use the concept of instance space. The most obvious example of geometric models is when all the features are numerical and can become coordinates in a Cartesian coordinate system. When we only have two or three features, they are easy to visualize. However, since many machine learning problems have hundreds or thousands of features, and therefore dimensions, visualizing these spaces is impossible. However, many of the geometric concepts, such as linear transformations, still apply in this hyper space. This can help us better understand our models. For instance, we expect that many learning algorithms will be translation invariant, that is, it does not matter where we place the origin in the coordinate system. Also, we can use the geometric concept of Euclidean distance to measure any similarities between instances; this gives us a method to cluster like instances and form a decision boundary between them.

Supposing we are using our linear classifier to classify paragraphs as either happy or sad and we have devised a set of tests. Each test is associated with a weight, w, to determine how much each test contributes to the overall result.

We can simply sum up each test and multiply it by its weight to get an overall score and create a decision rule that will create a boundary, for example, if the happy score is greater than a threshold, t.

$$\sum_{i=1}^{n} w_i x_i > t$$

Each feature contributes independently to the overall result, hence the rules linearity. This contribution depends on each feature's relative weight. This weight can be positive or negative, and each individual feature is not subject to the threshold while calculating the overall score.

We can rewrite this sum with vector notation using w for a vector of weights $(w_1, w_2, ..., w_n)$ and x for a vector of test results $(x_1, x_2, ..., x_n)$. Also, if we make it an equality, we can define the decision boundary:

$w . x = t$

We can think of w as a vector pointing between the "centers of mass" of the positive (happy) examples, P, and the negative examples, N. We can calculate these centers of mass by averaging the following:

$$P = \frac{1}{n}\sum pX \quad \text{and} \quad N = \frac{1}{n}\sum nX$$

Our aim now is to create a decision boundary half way between these centers of mass. We can see that w is proportional, or equal, to P - N, and that $(P + N)/2$ will be on the decision boundary. So, we can write the following:

$$t = (P - N) \cdot \frac{(P+N)}{2} = \frac{\left(\|P\|^2 - \|N\|^2 \right)}{2}$$

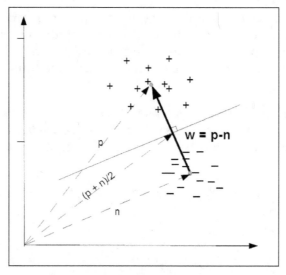

Fig of Decision boundary

In practice, real data is noisy and not necessarily that is easy to separate. Even when data is easily separable, a particular decision boundary may not have much meaning. Consider data that is sparse, such as in text classification where the number of words is large compared to the number of instances of each word. In this large area of empty instance space, it may be easy to find a decision boundary, but which is the best one? One way to choose is to use a margin to measure the distance between the decision boundary and its closest instance. We will explore these techniques later in the book.

Probabilistic models

A typical example of a probabilistic model is the Bayesian classifier, where you are given some training data (*D*), and a probability based on an initial training set (a particular hypothesis, *h*), getting the posteriori probability, *P (h/D)*.

$$P(h \mid D) = \frac{P(D \mid h)P(h)}{P(D)}$$

As an example, consider that we have a bag of marbles. We know that 40 percent of them are red and 60 percent are blue. We also know that half of the red marbles and all the blue marbles have flecks of white. When we reach into the bag to select a marble, we can feel by its texture that it has flecks. What are the chances of it being red?

Let *P(RF)* be equal to the probability that a randomly drawn marble with flecks is red:

P(FR) = the probability of a red marble with flecks is 0.5.

P(R) = the probability a marble being red is 0.4.

P(F) = the probability that a marble has flecks is *0.5 x 0.4 + 1 x 0.6= 0.8*.

$$P(R\,|\,F)=\frac{P(F\,|\,R)P(R)}{P(F)}=\frac{0.5X0.4}{0.8}=0.25$$

Probabilistic models allow us to explicitly calculate probabilities, rather than just a binary true or false. As we know, the key thing we need to do is create a model that maps or features a variable to a target variable. When we take a probabilistic approach, we assume that there is an underlying random process that creates a well defined but unknown probability distribution.

Consider a spam detector. Our feature variable, X, could consist of a set of words that indicate the email might be spam. The target variable, Y, is the instance class, either spam or ham. We are interested in the conditional probability of Y given X. For each email instance, there will be a feature vector, X, consisting of Boolean values representing the presence of our spam words. We are trying to find out whether Y, our target Boolean, is representing spam or not spam.

Now, consider that we have two words, x_1 and x_2, that constitute our feature vector X. From our training set, we can construct a table such as the following one:

	P(Y = spam | x_1, x_2)	P(Y = not spam | x_1, x_2)
P(Y | $x_1 = 0,\ x_2 = 0$)	0.1	0.9
P(Y | $x_1 = 0,\ x_2 = 1$)	0.7	0.3
P(Y | $x_1 = 1,\ x_2 = 0$)	0.4	0.6
P(Y | $x_1 = 1,\ x_2 = 1$)	0.8	0.2

Table 1.1

We can see that once we begin adding more words to our feature vector, it will quickly grow unmanageable. With a feature vector of n size, we will have 2^n cases to distinguish. Fortunately, there are other methods to deal with this problem, as we shall see later.

The probabilities in the preceding table are known as posterior probabilities. These are used when we have knowledge from a prior distribution. For instance, that one in ten emails is spam. However, consider a case where we may know that X contains $x_2 = 1$, but we are unsure of the value of x_1. This instance could belong in row 2, where the probability of it being spam is **0.7**, or in row 4, where the probability is **0.8**. The solution is to average these two rows using the probability of $x_1 = 1$ in any instance. That is, the probability that a word, x_1, will appear in any email, spam or not:

$P(Y|x_2 = 1) = P(Y|x_1 = 0, x_2 = 1)P(x_1 = 0) + P(x_1 = 1, x_2 = 1)P(x_1 = 1)$

This is called a likelihood function. If we know, from a training set, that the probability that x_1 is one is 0.1 then the probability that it is zero is 0.9 since these probabilities must sum to 1. So, we can calculate the probability that an e-mail contains the spam word $0.7 * 0.9 + 0.8 * 0.1 = 0.71$.

This is an example of a likelihood function: $P(X|Y)$. So, why do we want to know the probability of X, which is something we all ready know, conditioned on Y, which is something we know nothing about? A way to look at this is to consider the probability of any email containing a particular random paragraph, say, the 127th paragraph of War and Peace. Clearly, this probability is small, regardless of whether the e-mail is spam or not. What we are really interested in is not the magnitude of these likelihoods, but rather their ratio. How much more likely is an email containing a particular combination of words to be spam or not spam? These are sometimes called generative models because we can sample across all the variables involved.

We can use Bayes' rule to transform between prior distributions and a likelihood function:

$$P(YX) = \frac{P(XY)P(Y)}{P(X)}$$

$P(Y)$ is the prior probability, that is, how likely each class is, before having observed X. Similarly, $P(X)$ is the probability without taking into account Y. If we have only two classes, we can work with ratios. For instance, if we want to know how much the data favors each class, we can use the following:

$$\frac{P(Y = spam\,X)}{P(Y = ham\,X)} = \frac{P(X\,Y = spam)}{P(X\,Y = ham)}\frac{P(Y = spam)}{P(Y = ham)}$$

If the odds are less than one, we assume that the class in the denominator is the most likely. If it is greater than one, then the class in the enumerator is the most likely. If we use the data from *Table 1.1*, we calculate the following posterior odds:

$$\frac{P(Y = spam\,x_1 = 0, x_2 = 0)}{P(Y = ham\,x_1 = 0, x_2 = 0)} = \frac{0.1}{0.9} = 0.11$$

$$\frac{P(Y = spam\,x_1 = 1, x_2 = 1)}{P(Y = ham\,x_1 = 1, x_2 = 1)} = \frac{0.8}{0.2} = 0.4$$

$$\frac{P(Y = spam\,x_1 = 0, x_2 = 1)}{P(Y = ham\,x_1 = 0, x_2 = 1)} = \frac{0.7}{0.3} = 2.3$$

$$\frac{P(Y = spam\,x_1 = 1, x_2 = 0)}{P(Y = ham\,x_1 = 1, x_2 = 0)} = \frac{0.4}{0.6} = 0.66$$

The likelihood function is important in machine learning because it creates a generative model. If we know the probability distribution of each word in a vocabulary, together with the likelihood of each one appearing in either a spam or not spam e-mail, we can generate a random spam e-mail according to the conditional probability, $P(X\,|\,Y = spam)$.

Logical models

Logical models are based on algorithms. They can be translated into a set of formal rules that can be understood by humans. For example, if both x_1 and x_2 are 1 then the email is classified as spam.

These logical rules can be organized into a tree structure. In the following figure, we see that the instance space is iteratively partitioned at each branch. The leaves consist of rectangular areas (or hyper rectangles in the case of higher dimensions) representing segments of the instance space. Depending on the task we are solving, the leaves are labeled with a class, probability, real number, and so on.

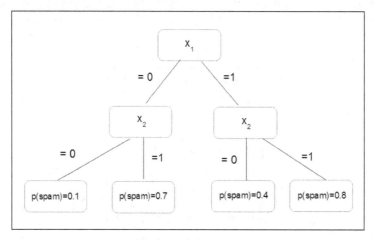

The figure feature tree

Feature trees are very useful when representing machine learning problems; even those that, at first sight, do not appear to have a tree structure. For instance, in the Bayes classifier in the previous section, we can partition our instance space into as many regions as there are combinations of feature values. Decision tree models often employ a pruning technique to delete branches that give an incorrect result. In *Chapter 3, Turning Data into Information*, we will look at a number of ways to represent decision trees in Python.

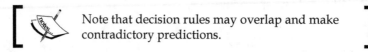

Note that decision rules may overlap and make contradictory predictions.

They are then said to be logically inconsistent. Rules can also be incomplete when they do not take into account all the coordinates in the feature space. There are a number of ways that we can address these issues, and we will look at these in detail later in the book.

Since tree learning algorithms usually work in a top down manner, the first task is to find a good feature to split on at the top of the tree. We need to find a split that will result in a higher degree of purity in subsequent nodes. By purity, I mean the degree to which training examples all belong to the same class. As we descend down the tree, at each level, we find the training examples at each node increase in purity, that is, they increasingly become separated into their own classes until we reach the leaf where all examples belong to the same class.

To look at this in another way, we are interested in lowering the entropy of subsequent nodes in our decision tree. Entropy, a measure of disorder, is high at the top of the tree (the root) and is progressively lowered at each node as the data is divided up into its respective classes.

In more complex problems, those with larger feature sets and decision rules, finding the optimum splits is sometimes not possible, at least not in an acceptable amount of time. We are really interested in creating the shallowest tree to reach our leaves in the shortest path. In the time it takes to analyze, each node grows exponentially with each additional feature, so the optimum decision tree may take longer to find than actually using a sub-optimum tree to perform the task.

An important property of logical models is that they can, to some extent, provide an explanation for their predictions. For example, consider the predictions made by a decision tree. By tracing the path from leaf to root we can determine the conditions that resulted in the final result. This is one of the advantages of logical models: they can be inspected by a human to reveal more about the problem.

Features

In the same way that decisions are only as good as the information available to us in real life, in a machine learning task, the model is only as good as its features. Mathematically, features are a function that maps from the instance space to a set of values in a particular domain. In machine learning, most measurements we make are numerical, and therefore the most common feature domain is the set of real numbers. Other common domains include Boolean, true or false, integers (say, when we are counting the occurrence of a particular feature), or finite sets such as a set of colors or shapes.

Models are defined in terms of their features. Also, single features can be turned into a model, which is known as a univariate model. We can distinguish between two uses of features. This is related to the distinction between grouping and grading.

Firstly, we can group our features by zooming into an area in the instance space. Let f be a feature counting the number of occurrences of a word, x_1, in an e-mail, X. We can set up conditions such as the following:

Where $f(X)=0$, representing emails that do not contain x_1 or where $f(X)>0$ representing emails that contain x_1 one or more times. These conditions are called **binary splits** because they divide the instance space into two groups: those that satisfy the condition and those that don't. We can also split the instance space into more than two segments to create non-binary splits. For instance, where $f(X) = 0; 0 < F(X) < 5; F(X) > 5$, and so on.

Secondly, we can grade our features to calculate the independent contribution each one makes to the overall result. Recall our simple linear classifier, the decision rule of the following form:

$$\sum_{i=1}^{n} w_i x_i < t$$

Since this rule is linear, each feature makes an independent contribution to the score of an instance. This contribution depends on w_i. If it is positive, then a positive x_i will increase the score. If w_i is negative, a positive x_i decreases the score. If w_i is small or zero, then the contribution it makes to the overall result is negligible. It can be seen that the features make a measurable contribution to the final prediction.

These two uses of features, as splits (grouping) and predictors (grading), can be combined into one model. A typical example occurs when we want to approximate a non-linear function, say $y \sin \pi x$, on the interval, $-1 < x < 1$. Clearly, the simple linear model will not work. Of course, the simple answer is to split the x axis into $-1 < x\ 0$ and $0 <$. On each of these segments, we can find a reasonable linear approximation.

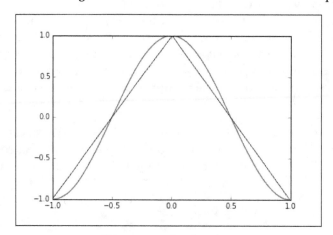

Using grouping and grading

A lot of work can be done to improve our model's performance by feature construction and transformation. In most machine learning problems, the features are not necessarily explicitly available. They need to be constructed from raw datasets and then transformed into something that our model can make use of. This is especially important in problems such as text classification. In our simple spam example, we used what is known as a bag of words representation because it disregards the order of the words. However, by doing this, we lose important information about the meaning of the text.

An important part of feature construction is discretization. We can sometimes extract more information, or information that is more relevant to our task, by dividing features into relevant chunks. For instance, supposing our data consists of a list of people's precise incomes, and we are trying to determine whether there is a relationship between financial income and the suburb a person lives in. Clearly, it would be appropriate if our feature set did not consist of precise incomes but rather ranges of income, although strictly speaking, we would lose information. If we choose our intervals appropriately, we will not lose information related to our problem, and our model will perform better and give us results that are easier to interpret.

This highlights the major tasks of feature selection: separating the signal from the noise.

Real world data will invariably contain a lot of information that we do not need, as well as just plain random noise, and separating the, perhaps small, part of the data that is relevant to our needs is important to the success of our model. It is of course important that we do not throw out information that may be important to us.

Often, our features will be non-linear, and linear regression may not give us good results. A trick is to transform the instance space itself. Supposing we have data such as what is shown in the following figure. Clearly, linear regression only gives us a reasonable fit, as shown in the figure on the left-hand side. However, we can improve this result if we square the instance space, that is, we make $x = x_2$ and $y = y_2$, as shown in the figure on the right-hand side:

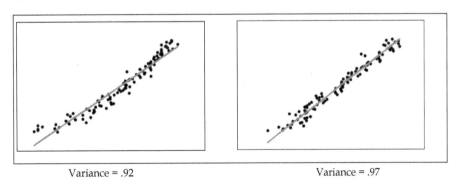

Variance = .92   Variance = .97

Transforming the instance space

We can go further and use a technique called the **kernel trick**. The idea is that we can create a higher dimensional implicit feature space. Pairs of data points are mapped from the raw dataset to this higher dimensional space via a specified function, sometimes called a **similarity function**.

For instance, let $x_1 = (x_1, y_1)$ and $x_2 = (x_2, y_2)$.

We create a 2D to 3D mapping, shown as follows:

$$(x, y) \square \left(x^2, y^2, \sqrt{2}xy \right)$$

The points in the 3D space corresponding to the 2D points, x_1 and x_2, are as follows:

$$x_1' = \left(x_1^2, y_1^2, \sqrt{2}x_1 y_1 \right) \quad \text{and} \quad x_2' = \left(x_2^2, y_2^2, \sqrt{2}x_2 y_2 \right)$$

Now, the dot product of these two vectors is:

$$x_1' \bullet x_2' = x_1^2 x_2^2 + y_1^2 y_2^2 + 2x_1 y_1 x_2 y_2 = \left(x_1 x_2 + y_1 y_2 \right) = \left(x_1 \bullet x_2 \right)^2$$

We can see that by squaring the dot product in the original 2D space, we obtain the dot product in the 3D space without actually creating the feature vectors themselves. Here, we have defined the kernel $k(x_1, x_2) = (x_1, x_2)2$. Calculating the dot product in a higher dimensional space is often computationally cheaper, and as we will see, this technique is used quite widely in machine learning from **Support Vector Machines (SVM)**, **Principle Component Analysis (PCA)**, and correlation analysis.

The basic linear classifier we looked at earlier defines a decision boundary, $w \bullet x = t$. The vector, w, is equal to the difference between the mean of the positive example and the mean of the negative examples, $p-n$. Suppose that we have the points $n = (0,0)$ and $p = (0,1)$. Let's assume that we have obtained a positive mean from two training examples, $p1 = (-1,1)$ and $p2 = (1,1)$. Therefore, we have the following:

$$p = \frac{1}{2} \left(p_1 + p_2 \right)$$

We can now write the decision boundary as the following:

$$\frac{1}{2} p_1 \bullet x + \frac{1}{2} p_2 \bullet x - n \bullet x = t$$

Using the kernel trick, we can obtain the following decision boundary:

$$\frac{1}{2}k(p_1,x)+\frac{1}{2}k(p_2,x)-k(n,x)=t$$

With the kernel we defined earlier, we get the following:

$$k(p_1,x)=(-x+y)^2,\ k(p_2,x)=(x+y)^2\ and\ k(n,x)=0$$

We can now derive the decision boundary:

$$\frac{1}{2}(-x+y)^2+\frac{1}{2}(x+y)^2=x^2+y^2$$

This is simply a circle around the origin with a radius $\sqrt{t}$.

Using the kernel trick, on the other hand, each new instance is evaluated against each training example. In return for this more complex calculation we obtain a more flexible non-linear decision boundary.

A very interesting and important aspect is the interaction between features. One form of interaction is correlation. For example, words in a blog post, where we might perhaps expect there to be a positive correlation between the words *winter* and *cold*, and a negative correlation between *winter* and *hot*. What this means for your model depends on your task. If you are doing a sentiment analysis, you might want to consider reducing the weights of each word if they appear together since the addition of another correlated word would be expected to contribute marginally less weight to the overall result than if that word appeared by itself.

Also with regards to sentiment analysis, we often need to transform certain features to capture their meaning. For example, the phrase *not happy* contains a word that would, if we just used *1-grams*, contribute to a positive sentiment score even though its sentiment is clearly negative. A solution (apart from using *2-grams*, which may unnecessarily complicate the model) would be to recognize when these two words appear in a sequence and create a new feature, *not_happy*, with an associated sentiment score.

Selecting and optimizing features is time well spent. It can be a significant part of the design of learning systems. This iterative nature of design flips between two phases. Firstly, understanding the properties of the phenomena you are studying, and secondly, testing your ideas with experimentation. This experimentation gives us deeper insight into the phenomena, allowing us to optimize our features and gain deeper understanding, among other things, until we are satisfied about our model giving us an accurate reflection of reality.

Unified modeling language

Machine learning systems can be complex. It is often difficult for a human brain to understand all the interactions of a complete system. We need some way to abstract the system into a set of discrete functional components. This enables us to visualize our system's structure and behavior with diagrams and plots.

UML is a formalism that allows us to visualize and communicate our design ideas in a precise way. We implement our systems in code, and the underlying principles are expressed in mathematics, but there is a third aspect, which is, in a sense, perpendicular to these, and that is a visual representation of our system. The process of drawing out your design helps conceptualize it from a different perspective. Perhaps we could consider trying to triangulate a solution.

Conceptual models are theoretical devices for describing elements of a problem. They can help us clarify assumptions, prove certain properties, and give us a fundamental understanding of the structures and interactions of systems.

UML arose out of the need to both simplify this complexity and allow our designs to be communicated clearly and unambiguously to team members, clients, and other stakeholders. A model is a simplified representation of a real system. Here, we use the word *model* in a more general sense, as compared to its more precise machine learning definition. UML can be used to model almost any system imaginable. The core idea is to strip away any irrelevant and potentially confusing elements with a clear representation of core attributes and functions.

Class diagrams

The class diagram models the static structure of a system. Classes represent abstract entities with common characteristics. They are useful because they express, and enforce, an object-oriented approach to our programming. We can see that by separating distinct objects in our code, we can work more clearly on each object as a self-contained unit. We can define it with a specific set of characteristics, and define how it relates to other objects. This enables complex programs to be broken down into separate functional components. It also allows us to subclass objects via inheritance. This is extremely useful and mirrors how we model the particularly hierarchical aspect of our world (that is, programmer is a subclass of *human*, and *Python programmer* is a subclass of programmer). Object programming can speed up the overall development time because it allows the reuse of components. There is a rich class library of developed components to draw upon. Also, the code produced tends to be easier to maintain because we can replace or change classes and are able to (usually) understand how this will affect the overall system.

In truth, object coding does tend to result in a larger code base, and this can mean that programs will be slower to run. In the end, it is not an "either, or" situation. For many simple tasks, you probably do not want to spend the time creating a class if you may never use it again. In general, if you find yourself typing the same bits of code, or creating the same type of data structures, it is probably a good idea to create a class. The big advantage of object programming is that we can encapsulate the data and the functions that operate on the data in one object. These software objects can correspond in quite a direct way with real world objects.

Designing object-oriented systems may take some time, initially. However, while establishing a workable class structure and class definitions, the coding tasks required to implement the class becomes clearer. Creating a class structure can be a very useful way to begin modeling a system. When we define a class, we are interested in a specific set of attributes, as a subset of all possible attributes or actual irrelevant attributes. It should be an accurate representation of a real system, and we need to make the judgment as to what is relevant and what is not. This is difficult because real world phenomena are complex, and the information we have about the system is always incomplete. We can only go by what we know, so our domain knowledge (the understanding of the system(s) we are trying to model), whether it be a software, natural, or human, is critically important.

Object diagrams

Object diagrams are a logical view of the system at runtime. They are a snapshot at a particular instant in time and can be understood as an instance of a class diagram. Many parameters and variables change value as the program is run, and the object diagram's function is to map these. This runtime binding is one of the key things object diagrams represent. By using links to tie objects together, we can model a particular runtime configuration. Links between objects correspond to associations between the objects class. So, the link is bound by the same constraints as the class that it enforces on its object.

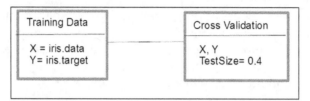

The object diagram

Both, the class diagram and the object diagram, are made of the same basic elements. While the class diagram represents an abstract blueprint of the class. The object diagram represents the real state of an object at a particular point in time. A single-object diagram cannot represent every class instance, so when drawing these diagrams, we must confine ourselves to the important instances and instances that cover the basic functionality of the system. The object diagram should clarify the association between objects and indicate the values of important variables.

Activity diagrams

The purpose of an activity diagram is to model the system's work flow by chaining together separate actions that together represent a process. They are particularly good at modeling sets of coordinated tasks. Activity diagrams are one of the most used in the UML specification because they are intuitive to understand as their formats are based on traditional flow chart diagrams. The main components of an activity diagram are actions, edges (sometimes called paths) and decisions. Actions are represented by rounded rectangles, edges are represented by arrows, and decisions are represented by a diamond. Activity diagrams usually have a start node and an end node.

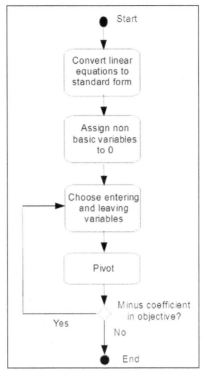

A figure of an example activity diagram

State diagrams

State diagrams are used to model systems that change behavior depending on what state they are in. They are represented by states and transitions. States are represented by rounded rectangles and transitions by arrows. Each transition has a trigger, and this is written along the arrow.

Many state diagrams will include an initial pseudo state and a final state. Pseudo states are states that control the flow of traffic. Another example is the choice pseudo state. This indicates that a Boolean condition determines a transition.

A state transition system consists of four elements; they are as follows:

- $S = \{s_1, s_2 \ldots\}$: A set of states
- $A = \{a_1, a_2 \ldots\}$: A set of actions
- $E = \{e_1, e_2 \ldots\}$: A set of events
- $y: S(A \cup E) \rightarrow 2s$: A state transition function

The first element, S, is the set of all possible states the world can be in. Actions are the things an agent can do to change the world. Events can happen in the world and are not under the control of an agent. The state transition function, y, takes two things as input: a state of the world and the union of actions and events. This gives us all the possible states as a result of applying a particular action or event.

Consider that we have a warehouse that stocks three items. We consider the warehouse only stocks, at most, one of each item. We can represent the possible states of the warehouse by the following matrix:

$$S = \begin{matrix} 0 & 1 & 0 & 1 & 0 & 0 & 1 & 1 \\ 0 & 0 & 1 & 1 & 1 & 0 & 0 & 1 \\ 0 & 0 & 0 & 0 & 1 & 1 & 1 & 1 \end{matrix}$$

This can define similar binary matrices for E, representing the event sold, and A, which is an action order.

In this simple example, our transition function is applied to an instance (s, which is a column in S), which is $s' = s + a - e$, where s' is the system's final state, s is its initial state, and a and e are an activity and an event respectively.

We can represent this with the following transition diagram:

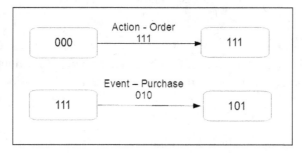

The figure of a transition Diagram

Summary

So far, we have introduced a broad cross-section of machine learning problems, techniques, and concepts. Hopefully by now, you have an idea of how to begin tackling a new and unique problem by breaking it up into its components. We have reviewed some of the essential mathematics and explored ways to visualize our designs. We can see that the same problem can have many different representations, and that each one may highlight different aspects. Before we can begin modeling, we need a well-defined objective, phrased as a specific, feasible, and meaningful question. We need to be clear how we can phrase the question in a way that a machine can understand.

The design process, although consisting of different and distinct activities, is not necessarily a linear process, but rather more of an iterative one. We cycle through each particular phase, proposing and testing ideas until we feel we can jump to the next phase. Sometimes we may jump back to a previous stage. We may sit at an equilibrium point, waiting for a particular event to occur; we may cycle through stages or go through several stages in parallel.

In the next chapter, we will begin our exploration of the practical tools that are available in the various Python libraries.

2
Tools and Techniques

Python comes equipped with a large library of packages for machine learning tasks.

The packages we will look at in this chapter are as follows:

- The IPython console
- NumPy, which is an extension that adds support for multi-dimensional arrays, matrices, and high-level mathematical functions
- SciPy, which is a library of scientific formulae, constants, and mathematical functions
- Matplotlib, which is for creating plots
- Scikit-learn, which is a library for machine learning tasks such as classification, regression, and clustering

There is only enough space to give you a *flavor* of these huge libraries, and an important skill is being able to find and understand the reference material for the various packages. It is impossible to present all the different functionality in a tutorial style documentation, and it is important to be able to find your way around the sometimes dense API references. A thing to remember is that the majority of these packages are put together by the open source community. They are not monolithic structures like you would expect from a commercial product, and therefore, understanding the various package taxonomies can be confusing. However, the diversity of approaches of open source software, and the fact that ideas are being contributed continually, give it an important advantage.

However, the evolving quality of open source software has its down side, especially for ML applications. For example, there was considerable reluctance on behalf of the Python machine learning user community to move from Python 2 to 3. Because Python 3 broke backwards compatibility; importantly, in terms of its numerical handling, it was not a trivial process to update the relevant packages. At the time of writing, all of the important (well important for me!) packages, and all those used in this book, were working with Python 2.7 or 3x. The major distributions of Python have Python 3 versions with a slightly different package set.

Python for machine learning

Python is a versatile general purpose programming language. It is an interpreted language and can run interactively from a console. It does not require a compiler like C++ or Java, so the development time tends to be shorter. It is available for free download and can be installed on many different operating systems including UNIX, Windows, and Macintosh. It is especially popular for scientific and mathematical applications. Python is relatively easy to learn compared to languages such as C++ and Java, with similar tasks using fewer lines of code.

Python is not the only platform for machine learning, but it is certainly one of the most used. One of its major alternatives is **R**. Like Python, it is open source, and while it is popular for applied machine learning, it lacks the large development community of Python. R is a specialized tool for machine learning and statistical analysis. Python is a general-purpose, widely-used programming language that also has excellent libraries for machine learning applications.

Another alternative is **Matlab**. Unlike R and Python, it is a commercial product. As would be expected, it contains a polished user interface and exhaustive documentation. Like R, however, it lacks the versatility of Python. Python is such an incredibly useful language that your effort to learn it, compared to the other platforms, will provide far greater pay-offs. It also has excellent libraries for network, web development, and microcontroller programming. These applications can complement or enhance your work in machine learning, all without the pain of clumsy integrations and the learning or remembering of the specifics of different languages.

IPython console

The Ipython package has had some significant changes with the release of version 4. A former monolithic package structure, it has been split into sub-packages. Several IPython projects have split into their own separate project. Most of the repositories have been moved to the **Jupyter** project (jupyter.org).

At the core of IPython is the IPython console: a powerful interactive interpreter that allows you to test your ideas in a very fast and intuitive way. Instead of having to create, save, and run a file every time you want to test a code snippet, you can simply type it into a console. A powerful feature of IPython is that it decouples the traditional read-evaluate-print loop that most computing platforms are based on. IPython puts the evaluate phase into its own process: a kernel (not to be confused with the kernel function used in machine learning algorithms). Importantly, more than one client can access the kernel. This means you can run code in a number of files and access them, for example, running a method from the console. Also, the kernel and the client do not need to be on the same machine. This has powerful implications for distributed and networked computing.

The IPython console adds command-line features, such as tab completion and `%magic` commands, which replicate terminal commands. If you are not using a distribution of Python with IPython already installed, you can start IPython by typing `ipython` into a Python command line. Typing `%quickref` into the IPython console will give you a list of commands and their function.

The IPython notebook should also be mentioned. The notebook has merged into another project known as Jupyter (`jupyter.org`). This web application is a powerful platform for numerical computing in over 40 languages. The notebook allows you to share and collaborate on live code and publish rich graphics and text.

Installing the SciPy stack

The **SciPy** stack consists of Python along with the most commonly used scientific, mathematical, and ML libraries. (visit: `scipy.org`). These include **NumPy**, **Matplotlib**, the SciPy library itself, and IPython. The packages can be installed individually on top of an existing Python installation, or as a complete distribution (**distro**). The easiest way to get started is using a distro, if you have not got Python installed on your computer. The major Python distributions are available for most platforms, and they contain everything you need in one package. Installing all the packages and their dependencies separately does take some time, but it may be an option if you already have a configured Python installation on your machine.

Most distributions give you all the tools you need, and many come with powerful developer environments. Two of the best are **Anaconda** (`www.continuum.io/downloads`) and **Canopy** (`http://www.enthought.com/products/canopy/`). Both have free and commercial versions. For reference, I will be using the Anaconda distribution of Python.

Installing the major distributions is usually a pretty painless task.

 Be aware that not all distributions include the same set of Python modules, and you may have to install modules, or reinstall the correct version of a module.

NumPY

We should know that there is a hierarchy of types for representing data in Python. At the root are immutable objects such as integers, floats, and Boolean. Built on this, we have sequence types. These are ordered sets of objects indexed by non-negative integers. They are iterative objects that include strings, lists, and tuples. Sequence types have a common set of operations such as returning an element (*s[i]*) or a slice (*s[i:j]*), and finding the length (*len(s)*) or the sum (*sum(s)*). Finally, we have mapping types. These are collections of objects indexed by another collection of key objects. Mapping objects are unordered and are indexed by numbers, strings, or other objects. The built-in Python mapping type is the dictionary.

NumPy builds on these data objects by providing two further objects: an N-dimensional array object (ndarray) and a universal function object (ufunc). The ufunc object provides element-by-element operations on ndarray objects, allowing typecasting and array broadcasting. Typecasting is the process of changing one data type into another, and broadcasting describes how arrays of different sizes are treated during arithmetic operations. There are sub-packages for linear algebra (linalg), random number generation (random), discrete Fourier transforms (fft), and unit testing (testing).

NumPy uses a dtype object to describe various aspects of the data. This includes types of data such as float, integer, and so on, the number of bytes in the data type (if the data is structured), and also, the names of the fields and the shape of any sub arrays. NumPy has several new data types, including the following:

- 8, 16, 32, and 64 bit int values
- 16, 32, and 64 bit float values
- 64 and 128 bit complex types
- Ndarray structured array types

We can convert between types using the `np.cast` object. This is simply a dictionary that is keyed according to destination cast type, and whose value is the appropriate function to perform the casting. Here we cast an integer to a float32:

f= np.cast['f'] (2)

NumPy arrays can be created in several ways such as converting them from other Python data structures, using the built-in array creation objects such as `arange()`, `ones()` and `zeros()`, or from files such as `.csv` or `.html`.

`Indexing` and `slicingNumPy` builds on the slicing and indexing techniques used in sequences. You should already be familiar with slicing sequences, such as lists and tuples, in Python using the `[i:j:k]` syntax, where `i` is the start index, `j` is the end, and `k` is the step. NumPy extends this concept of the selection tuple to N-dimensions.

Fire up a Python console and type the following commands:

```
import numpy as np
a=np.arange(60).reshape(3,4,5)
print(a)
```

You will observe the following:

```
array([[[ 0,  1,  2,  3,  4],
        [ 5,  6,  7,  8,  9],
        [10, 11, 12, 13, 14],
        [15, 16, 17, 18, 19]],

       [[20, 21, 22, 23, 24],
        [25, 26, 27, 28, 29],
        [30, 31, 32, 33, 34],
        [35, 36, 37, 38, 39]],

       [[40, 41, 42, 43, 44],
        [45, 46, 47, 48, 49],
        [50, 51, 52, 53, 54],
        [55, 56, 57, 58, 59]]])
```

This will print the preceding 3 by 4 by 5 array. You should know that we can access each item in the array using a notation such as `a[2,3,4]`. This returns `59`. Remember that indexing begins at 0.

We can use the slicing technique to return a slice of the array.

The following image shows the `A[1:2:]` array:

```
array([[[20, 21, 22, 23, 24],
        [25, 26, 27, 28, 29],
        [30, 31, 32, 33, 34],
        [35, 36, 37, 38, 39]]])
```

Using the ellipse (...), we can select any remaining unspecified dimensions. For example, `a[...,1]` is equivalent to `a[:,:,1]`:

```
array([[ 1,  6, 11, 16],
       [21, 26, 31, 36],
       [41, 46, 51, 56]])
```

You can also use negative numbers to count from the end of the axis:

```
In [5]: a[-1:,:,-5]
Out[5]: array([[40, 45, 50, 55]])
```

With slicing, we are creating views; the original array remains untouched, and the view retains a reference to the original array. This means that when we create a slice, even though we assign it to a new variable, if we change the original array, these changes are also reflected in the new array. The following figure demonstrates this:

```
In [6]: b=a[2,2,0:2]

In [7]: b
Out[7]: array([50, 51])

In [8]: a[2]=0 #changing a changes b

In [9]: b
Out[9]: array([0, 0])
```

Here, **a** and **b** are referring to the same array. When we assign values in a, this is also reflected in b. To copy an array rather than simply make a reference to it, we use the deep `copy()` function from the `copy` package in the standard library:

```
import copy
```

```
c=copy.deepcopy(a)
```

Here, we have created a new independent array, c. Any changes made in array a will not be reflected in array c.

Constructing and transforming arrays

This slicing functionality can also be used with several NumPy classes as an efficient means of constructing arrays. The `numpy.mgrid` object, for example, creates a `meshgrid` object, which provides, in certain circumstances, a more convenient alternative to `arange()`. Its primary purpose is to build a coordinate array for a specified N-dimensional volume. Refer to the following figure as an example:

```
In [10]: np.mgrid[0:4,0:4]
Out[10]:
array([[[0, 0, 0, 0],
        [1, 1, 1, 1],
        [2, 2, 2, 2],
        [3, 3, 3, 3]],

       [[0, 1, 2, 3],
        [0, 1, 2, 3],
        [0, 1, 2, 3],
        [0, 1, 2, 3]]])
```

Sometimes, we will need to manipulate our data structures in other ways. These include:

- **concatenating**: By using the `np.r_` and `np.c_` functions, we can concatenate along one or two axes using the slicing constructs. Here is an example:

```
In [11]: np.r_[-2,-1:5j,2]
Out[11]: array([-2.+0.j, -1.+0.j,  2.+0.j])
```

  Here we have used the complex number **5j** as the step size, which is interpreted by Python as the number of points, inclusive, to fit between the specified range, which here is **-1** to **1**.

- **newaxis**: This object expands the dimensions of an array:

```
In [12]: a[np.newaxis,:,:].shape
Out[12]: (1, 3, 4, 5)
```

  This creates an extra axis in the first dimension. The following creates the new axis in the second dimension:

```
In [13]: a[:,np.newaxis,:].shape
Out[13]: (3, 1, 4, 5)
```

You can also use a Boolean operator to filter:

```
a[a<5]
Out[]: array([0, 1, 2, 3, 4])
```

- Find the sum of a given axis:

```
In [14]: a.sum(2)
Out[14]:
array([[ 10,  35,  60,  85],
       [110, 135, 160, 185],
       [  0,   0,   0,   0]])
```

Here we have summed using axis 2.

Mathematical operations

As you would expect, you can perform mathematical operations such as addition, subtraction, multiplication, as well as the trigonometric functions on NumPy arrays. Arithmetic operations on different shaped arrays can be carried out by a process known as **broadcasting**. When operating on two arrays, NumPy compares their shapes element-wise from the trailing dimension. Two dimensions are compatible if they are the same size, or if one of them is 1. If these conditions are not met, then a ValueError exception is thrown.

This is all done in the background using the ufunc object. This object operates on ndarrays on a element-by-element basis. They are essentially wrappers that provide a consistent interface to scalar functions to allow them to work with NumPy arrays. There are over 60 ufunc objects covering a wide variety of operations and types. The ufunc objects are called automatically when you perform operations such as adding two arrays using the + operator.

Let's look into some additional mathematical features:

- **Vectors**: We can also create our own vectorized versions of scalar functions using the np.vectorize() function. It takes a Python scalar function or method as a parameter and returns a vectorized version of this function:

```
def myfunc(a,b):
def myfunc(a,b):
if a > b:
        return a-b
    else:
        return a + b
vfunc=np.vectorize(myfunc)
```

We will observe the following output:

```
In [18]: vfunc([1,2,3,4],[4,3,2,1])
Out[18]: array([5, 5, 1, 3])
```

- **Polynomial functions**: The `poly1d` class allows us to deal with polynomial functions in a natural way. It accepts as a parameter an array of coefficients in decreasing powers. For example, the polynomial, $2x^2 + 3x + 4$, can be entered by the following:

```
In [27]: p=np.poly1d([2,3,4])

In [28]: print(np.poly1d(p))
   2
2 x + 3 x + 4
```

We can see that it prints out the polynomial in a human-readable way. We can perform various operations on the polynomial, such as evaluating at a point:

```
In [29]: p(3)
Out[29]: 31
```

- Find the roots:

```
In [30]: p.r
Out[30]: array([-0.75+1.19895788j,
-0.75-1.19895788j])
```

We can use `asarray(p)` to give the coefficients of the polynomial an array so that it can be used in all functions that accept arrays.

As we will see, the packages that are built on NumPy give us a powerful and flexible framework for machine learning.

Matplotlib

Matplotlib, or more importantly, its sub-package `PyPlot`, is an essential tool for visualizing two-dimensional data in Python. I will only mention it briefly here because its use should become apparent as we work through the examples. It is built to work like Matlab with command style functions. Each `PyPlot` function makes some change to a `PyPlot` instance. At the core of `PyPlot` is the `plot` method. The simplest implementation is to pass plot a list or a 1D array. If only one argument is passed to plot, it assumes it is a sequence of y values, and it will automatically generate the x values. More commonly, we pass plot two 1D arrays or lists for the co-ordinates x and y. The `plot` method can also accept an argument to indicate line properties such as line width, color, and style. Here is an example:

```python
import numpy as np
import matplotlib.pyplot as plt


x = np.arange(0., 5., 0.2)
plt.plot(x, x**4, 'r', x, x*90, 'bs', x, x**3, 'g^')
plt.show()
```

This code prints three lines in different styles: a red line, blue squares, and green triangles. Notice that we can pass more than one pair of coordinate arrays to plot multiple lines. For a full list of line styles, type the `help(plt.plot)` function.

Pyplot, like Matlab, applies plotting commands to the current axes. Multiple axes can be created using the `subplot` command. Here is an example:

```python
x1 = np.arange(0., 5., 0.2)
x2 = np.arange(0., 5., 0.1)


plt.figure(1)
plt.subplot(211)
plt.plot(x1, x1**4, 'r', x1, x1*90, 'bs', x1, x1**3, 'g^',linewidth=2.0)


plt.subplot(212)
plt.plot(x2,np.cos(2*np.pi*x2), 'k')
plt.show()
```

The output of the preceding code is as follows:

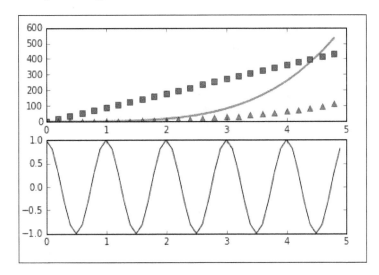

Another useful plot is the histogram. The `hist()` object takes an array, or a sequence of arrays, of input values. The second parameter is the number of bins. In this example, we have divided a distribution into 10 bins. The normed parameter, when set to 1 or `true`, normalizes the counts to form a probability density. Notice also that in this code, we have labeled the *x* and *y* axis, and displayed a title and some text at a location given by the coordinates:

```
mu, sigma = 100, 15
x = mu + sigma * np.random.randn(1000)
n, bins, patches = plt.hist(x, 10, normed=1, facecolor='g')
plt.xlabel('Frequency')
plt.ylabel('Probability')
plt.title('Histogram Example')
plt.text(40,.028, 'mean=100 std.dev.=15')
plt.axis([40, 160, 0, 0.03])
plt.grid(True)
plt.show()
```

The output for this code will look like this:

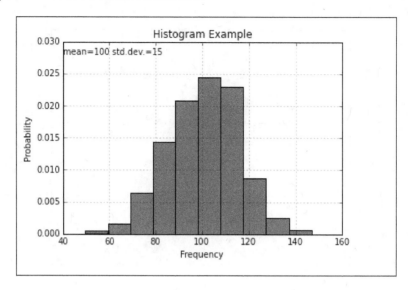

The final 2D plot we are going to look at is the scatter plot. The `scatter` object takes two sequence objects, such as arrays, of the same length and optional parameters to denote color and style attributes. Let's take a look at this code:

```
N = 100
x = np.random.rand(N)
y = np.random.rand(N)
#colors = np.random.rand(N)
colors=('r','b','g')
area = np.pi * (10 * np.random.rand(N))**2   # 0 to 10 point radiuses
plt.scatter(x, y, s=area, c=colors, alpha=0.5)
plt.show()
```

We will observe the following output:

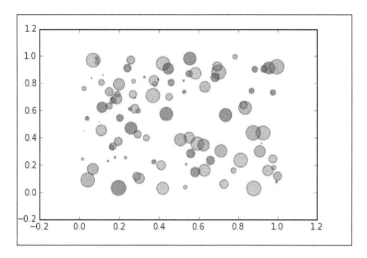

Matplotlib also has a powerful toolbox for rendering 3D plots. The following code demonstrations are simple examples of 3D line, scatter, and surface plots. 3D plots are created in a very similar way to 2D plots. Here, we get the current axis with the gca function and set the projection parameter to 3D. All the plotting methods work much like their 2D counterparts, except that they now take a third set of input values for the *z* axis:

```
import matplotlib as mpl
from mpl_toolkits.mplot3d import Axes3D
import numpy as np
import matplotlib.pyplot as plt
from matplotlib import cm

mpl.rcParams['legend.fontsize'] = 10

fig = plt.figure()
ax = fig.gca(projection='3d')
theta = np.linspace(-3 * np.pi, 6 * np.pi, 100)
z = np.linspace(-2, 2, 100)
r = z**2 + 1
x = r * np.sin(theta)
y = r * np.cos(theta)
ax.plot(x, y, z)
```

```
theta2 = np.linspace(-3 * np.pi, 6 * np.pi, 20)
z2 = np.linspace(-2, 2, 20)
r2=z2**2 +1
x2 = r2 * np.sin(theta2)
y2 = r2 * np.cos(theta2)

ax.scatter(x2,y2,z2, c= 'r')
x3 = np.arange(-5, 5, 0.25)
y3 = np.arange(-5, 5, 0.25)
x3, y3 = np.meshgrid(x3, y3)
R = np.sqrt(x3**2 + y3**2)
z3 = np.sin(R)
surf = ax.plot_surface(x3,y3,z3, rstride=1, cstride=1, cmap=cm.Greys_r,
                    linewidth=0, antialiased=False)
ax.set_zlim(-2, 2)
plt.show()
```

We will observe this output:

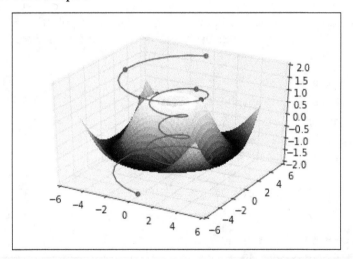

Pandas

The **Pandas** library builds on NumPy by introducing several useful data structures and functionalities to read and process data. Pandas is a great tool for general data munging. It easily handles common tasks such as dealing with missing data, manipulating shapes and sizes, converting between data formats and structures, and importing data from different sources.

The main data structures introduced by Pandas are:

- Series
- The DataFrame
- Panel

The DataFrame is probably the most widely used. It is a two-dimensional structure that is effectively a table created from either a NumPy array, lists, dicts, or series. You can also create a DataFrame by reading from a file.

Probably the best way to get a feel for Pandas is to go through a typical use case. Let's say that we are given the task of discovering how the daily maximum temperature has changed over time. For this example, we will be working with historical weather observations from the Hobart weather station in Tasmania. Download the following ZIP file and extract its contents into a folder called **data** in your Python working directory:

```
http://davejulian.net/mlbook/data_
```

The first thing we do is create a DataFrame from it:

```
import pandas as pd
df=pd.read_csv('data/sampleData.csv')
```

Check the first few rows in this data:

```
df.head()
```

We can see that the product code and the station number are the same for each row and that this information is superfluous. Also, the days of accumulated maximum temperature are not needed for our purpose, so we will delete them as well:

```
del df['Bureau of Meteorology station number']
del df['Product code']
del df['Days of accumulation of maximum temperature']
```

Let's make our data a little easier to read by shorting the column labels:

```
df=df.rename(columns={'Maximum temperature (Degree C)':'maxtemp'})
```

We are only interested in data that is of high quality, so we include only records that have a *Y* in the quality column:

```
df=df[(df.Quality=='Y')]
```

We can get a statistical summary of our data:

df.describe()

```
             Year         Month          Day        maxtemp
count  44250.000000  44250.000000  44250.000000  44250.000000
mean    1952.207503      6.536339     15.734870     16.929941
std       38.212270      3.446311      8.802089      5.030362
min     1882.000000      1.000000      1.000000      4.300000
25%     1924.000000      4.000000      8.000000     13.300000
50%     1954.000000      7.000000     16.000000     16.400000
75%     1985.000000     10.000000     23.000000     20.000000
max     2015.000000     12.000000     31.000000     41.800000
```

If we import the matplotlib.pyplot package, we can graph the data:

import matplotlib.pyplot as plt

plt.plot(df.Year, df.maxtemp)

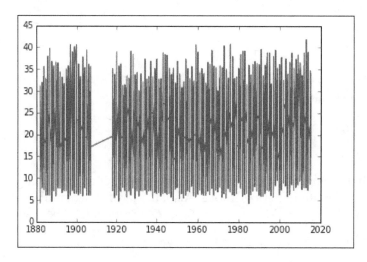

Notice that PyPlot correctly formats the date axis and deals with the missing data by connecting the two known points on either side. We can convert a DataFrame into a NumPy array using the following:

ndarray = df.values

If the DataFrame contains a mixture of data types, then this function will convert them to the lowest common denominator type, which means that the one that accommodates all values will be chosen. For example, if the DataFrame consists of a mix of float16 and float32 types, then the values will be converted to float 32.

The Pandas DataFrame is a great object for viewing and manipulating simple text and numerical data. However, Pandas is probably not the right tool for more sophisticated numerical processing such as calculating the dot product, or finding the solutions to linear systems. For numerical applications, we generally use the NumPy classes.

SciPy

SciPy (pronounced sigh pi) adds a layer to NumPy that wraps common scientific and statistical applications on top of the more purely mathematical constructs of NumPy. SciPy provides higher-level functions for manipulating and visualizing data, and it is especially useful when using Python interactively. SciPy is organized into sub-packages covering different scientific computing applications. A list of the packages most relevant to ML and their functions appear as follows:

Package	Description
cluster	This contains two sub-packages: cluster.vq for K-means clustering and vector quantization. cluster.hierachy for hierarchical and agglomerative clustering, which is useful for distance matrices, calculating statistics on clusters, as well as visualizing clusters with dendrograms.
constants	These are physical and mathematical constants such as *pi* and *e*.
integrate	These are differential equation solvers
interpolate	These are interpolation functions for creating new data points within a range of known points.
io	This refers to input and output functions for creating string, binary, or raw data streams, and reading and writing to and from files.
optimize	This refers to optimizing and finding roots.
linalg	This refers to linear algebra routines such as basic matrix calculations, solving linear systems, finding determinants and norms, and decomposition.
ndimage	This is N-dimensional image processing.
odr	This is orthogonal distance regression.
stats	This refers to statistical distributions and functions.

Many of the NumPy modules have the same name and similar functionality as those in the SciPy package. For the most part, SciPy imports its NumPy equivalent and extends its functionality. However, be aware that some identically named functions in SciPy modules may have slightly different functionality compared to those in NumPy. It also should be mentioned that many of the SciPy classes have convenience wrappers in the scikit-learn package, and it is sometimes easier to use those instead.

Each of these packages requires an explicit import; here is an example:

```
import scipy.cluster
```

You can get documentation from the SciPy website (`scipy.org`) or from the console, for example, `help(sicpy.cluster)`.

As we have seen, a common task in many different ML settings is that of optimization. We looked at the mathematics of the simplex algorithm in the last chapter. Here is the implementation using SciPy. We remember simplex optimizes a set of linear equations. The problem we looked at was as follows:

Maximize $x_1 + x_2$ within the constraints of: $2x_1 + x_2 \le 4$ and $x_1 + 2x_2 \le 3$

The `linprog` object is probably the simplest object that will solve this problem. It is a minimization algorithm, so we reverse the sign of our objective.

From `scipy.optimize`, import `linprog`:

```
objective=[-1,-1]
con1=[[2,1],[1,2]]
con2=[4,3]
res=linprog(objective,con1,con2)
print(res)
```

You will observe the following output:

```
      nit: 2
  message: 'Optimization terminated successfully.'
   status: 0
        x: array([ 1.66666667,  0.66666667])
  success: True
      fun: -2.3333333333333335
    slack: array([ 0.,  0.])
```

There is also an `optimisation.minimize` object that is suitable for slightly more complicated problems. This object takes a solver as a parameter. There are currently about a dozen solvers available, and if you need a more specific solver, you can write your own. The most commonly used, and suitable for most problems, is the **nelder-mead** solver. This particular solver uses a **downhill simplex** algorithm that is basically a heuristic search that replaces each test point with a high error with a point located in the centroid of the remaining points. It iterates through this process until it converges on a minimum.

In this example, we use the **Rosenbrock** function as our test problem. This is a non-convex function that is often used to test optimization problems. The global minimum of this function is on a long parabolic valley, and this makes it challenging for an algorithm to find the minimum in a large, relatively flat valley. We will see more of this function:

```python
import numpy as np
from scipy.optimize import minimize
def rosen(x):
    return sum(100.0*(x[1:]-x[:-1]**2.0)**2.0 + (1-x[:-1])**2.0)


def nMin(funct,x0):

    return(minimize(rosen, x0, method='nelder-mead', options={'xtol':
        1e-8, 'disp': True}))


x0 = np.array([1.3, 0.7, 0.8, 1.9, 1.2])


nMin(rosen,x0)
```

The output for the preceding code is as follows:

```
Optimization terminated successfully.
         Current function value: 0.000000
         Iterations: 339
         Function evaluations: 571
```

The minimize function takes two mandatory parameters. These are the objective function and the initial value of x0. The minimize function also takes an optional parameter for the solver method, in this example we use the `nelder-mead` method. The options are a solver-specific set of key-value pairs, represented as a dictionary. Here, `xtol` is the relative error acceptable for convergence, and `disp` is set to print a message. Another package that is extremely useful for machine learning applications is `scipy.linalg`. This package adds the ability to perform tasks such as inverting matrices, calculating eigenvalues, and matrix decomposition.

Scikit-learn

This includes algorithms for the most common machine learning tasks, such as classification, regression, clustering, dimensionality reduction, model selection, and preprocessing.

Scikit-learn comes with several real-world data sets for us to practice with. Let's take a look at one of these—the Iris data set:

```
from sklearn import datasets
iris = datasets.load_iris()
iris_X = iris.data
iris_y = iris.target
iris_X.shape
(150, 4)
```

The data set contains 150 samples of three types of irises (Setosa, Versicolor, and Virginica), each with four features. We can get a description on the dataset:

```
iris.DESCR
```

We can see that the four attributes, or features, are sepal width, sepal length, petal length, and petal width in centimeters. Each sample is associated with one of three classes. Setosa, Versicolor, and Virginica. These are represented by 0, 1, and 2 respectively.

Let's look at a simple classification problem using this data. We want to predict the type of iris based on its features: the length and width of its sepal and petals. Typically, scikit-learn uses estimators to implement a `fit(X, y)` method and for training a classifier, and a `predict(X)` method that if given unlabeled observations, X, returns the predicted labels, y. The `fit()` and `predict()` methods usually take a 2D array-like object.

Here, we are going to use the **K Nearest Neighbors (K-NN)** technique to solve this classification problem. The principle behind K-NN is relatively simple. We classify an unlabeled sample according to the classification of its nearest neighbors. Each data point is assigned class membership according to the majority class of a small number, *k*, of its nearest neighbors. K-NN is an example of instanced-based learning, where classification is not done according to an inbuilt model, but with reference to a labeled test set. The K-NN algorithm is known as non generalizing, since it simply remembers all its training data and compares it to each new sample. Despite, or perhaps because of, its apparent simplicity, K-NN is a very well used technique for solving a variety of classification and regression problems.

There are two different K-NN classifiers in **Sklearn**. **KNeighborsClassifier** requires the user to specify *k*, the number of nearest neighbors. **RadiusNeighborsClassifier**, on the other hand, implements learning based on the number of neighbors within a fixed radius, *r*, of each training point. KNeighborsClassifier is the more commonly used one. The optimal value for *k* is very much dependent on the data. In general, a larger *k* value is used with noisy data. The trade off being the classification boundary becomes less distinct. If the data is not uniformly sampled, then RadiusNeighborsClassifier may be a better choice. Since the number of neighbors is based on the radius, *k* will be different for each point. In sparser areas, *k* will be lower than in areas of high sample density:

```python
from sklearn.neighbors import KNeighborsClassifier as knn
from sklearn import datasets
import numpy as np
import matplotlib.pyplot as plt
from matplotlib.colors import ListedColormap


def knnDemo(X,y, n):

    #cresates the the classifier and fits it to the data
    res=0.05
    k1 = knn(n_neighbors=n,p=2,metric='minkowski')
    k1.fit(X,y)

    #sets up the grid
    x1_min, x1_max = X[:, 0].min() - 1, X[:, 0].max() + 1
    x2_min, x2_max = X[:, 1].min() - 1, X[:, 1].max() + 1
    xx1, xx2 = np.meshgrid(np.arange(x1_min, x1_max, res),np.arange(x2_min, x2_max, res))
```

```
#makes the prediction
Z = k1.predict(np.array([xx1.ravel(), xx2.ravel()]).T)
Z = Z.reshape(xx1.shape)

#creates the color map
cmap_light = ListedColormap(['#FFAAAA', '#AAFFAA', '#AAAAFF'])
cmap_bold = ListedColormap(['#FF0000', '#00FF00', '#0000FF'])

#Plots the decision surface
plt.contourf(xx1, xx2, Z, alpha=0.4, cmap=cmap_light)
plt.xlim(xx1.min(), xx1.max())
plt.ylim(xx2.min(), xx2.max())

#plots the samples
for idx, cl in enumerate(np.unique(y)):
    plt.scatter(X[:, 0], X[:, 1], c=y, cmap=cmap_bold)

plt.show()
```

```
iris = datasets.load_iris()
X1 = iris.data[:, 0:3:2]
X2 = iris.data[:, 0:2]
X3 = iris.data[:,1:3]
y = iris.target
knnDemo(X2,y,15)
```

Here is the output of the preceding commands:

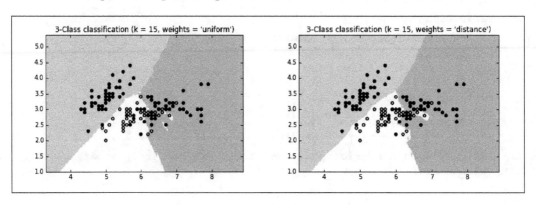

Let's now look at regression problems with Sklearn. The simplest solution is to minimize the sum of the squared error. This is performed by the `LinearRegression` object. This object has a `fit()` method that takes two vectors: *X*, the feature vector, and *y*, the target vector:

```
from sklearn import linear_model
clf = linear_model.LinearRegression()
clf.fit ([[0, 0], [1, 1], [2, 2]], [0, 1, 2])
clf.coef_
array([ 0.5,   0.5])
```

The `LinearRegression` object has four optional parameters:

- `fit_intercept`: A Boolean, which if set to `false`, will assume that the data is centered, and the model will not use an intercept in its calculation. The default value is `true`.

- `normalize`: If `true`, *X* will be normalized to zero mean and unit variance before regression. This is sometimes useful because it can make interpreting the coefficients a little more explicit. The default is `false`.

- `copy_X`: Defaults to `true`. If set to `false`, it will allow *X* to be overwritten.

- `n_jobs`: Is the number of jobs to use for the computation. This defaults to `1`. This can be used to speed up computation for large problems on multiple CPUs.

Its output has the following attributes:

- `coef_`: An array of the estimated coefficients for the linear regression problem. If y is multidimensional, that is there are multiple target variables, then `coef_` will be a 2D array of the form (n_targets, n_features). If only one target variable is passed, then `coef_` will be a 1D array of length (n_features).

- `intercept_`: This is an array of the intercept or independent terms in the linear model.

For the **Ordinary Least Squares** to work, we assume that the features are independent. When these terms are correlated, then the matrix, *X*, can approach singularity. This means that the estimates become highly sensitive to small changes in the input data. This is known as **multicollinearity** and results in a large variance and ultimately instability. We discuss this in greater detail later, but for now, let's look at an algorithm that, to some extent, addresses these issues.

Ridge regression not only addresses the issue of multicollinearity, but also situations where the number of input variables greatly exceeds the number of samples. The `linear_model.Ridge()` object uses what is known as L2 regularization. Intuitively, we can understand this as adding a penalty on the extreme values of the weight vector. This is sometimes called **shrinkage** because it makes the average weights smaller. This tends to make the model more stable because it reduces its sensitivity to extreme values.

The Sklearn object, `linear_model.ridge`, adds a regularization parameter, `alpha`. Generally, small positive values for `alpha` improves the model's stability. It can either be a float or an array. If it is an array, it is assumed that the array corresponds to specific targets, and therefore, it must be the same size as the target. We can try this out with the following simple function:

```python
from sklearn.linear_model import Ridge
import numpy as np

def ridgeReg(alpha):

    n_samples, n_features = 10, 5
    y = np.random.randn(n_samples)
    X = np.random.randn(n_samples, n_features)
    clf = Ridge(.001)
    res=clf.fit(X, y)
    return(res)
res= ridgeReg(0.001)
print (res.coef_)
print (res.intercept_)
```

Let's now look at some scikit-learn algorithms for dimensionality reduction. This is important for machine learning because it reduces the number of input variables or features that a model has to consider. This makes a model more efficient and can make the results easier to interpret. It can also increase a model's generalization by reducing overfitting.

It is important, of course, to not discard information that will reduce the accuracy of the model. Determining what is redundant or irrelevant is the major function of dimensionality reduction algorithms. There are basically two approaches: feature extraction and feature selection. Feature selection attempts to find a subset of the original feature variables. Feature extraction, on the other hand, creates new feature variables by combining correlated variables.

Let's first look at probably the most common feature extraction algorithm, that is, **Principle Component Analysis** or **PCA**. This uses an orthogonal transformation to convert a set of correlated variables into a set of uncorrelated variables. The important information, the length of vectors, and the angle between them does not change. This information is defined in the inner product and is preserved in an orthogonal transformation. PCA constructs a feature vector in such a way that the first component accounts for as much of the variability in the data as possible. Subsequent components then account for decreasing amounts of variability. This means that, for many models, we can just choose the first few principle components until we are satisfied that they account for as much variability in our data as is required by the experimental specifications.

Probably the most versatile kernel function, and the one that gives good results in most situations, is the **Radial Basis Function** (**RBF**). The rbf kernel takes a parameter, gamma, which can be loosely interpreted as the inverse of the sphere of influence of each sample. A low value of gamma means that each sample has a large radius of influence on samples selected by the model. The KernalPCA fit_transform method takes the training vector, fits it to the model, and then transforms it into its principle components. Let's look at the commands:

```python
import numpy as np
import matplotlib.pyplot as plt
from sklearn.decomposition import KernelPCA
from sklearn.datasets import make_circles
np.random.seed(0)
X, y = make_circles(n_samples=400, factor=.3, noise=.05)
kpca = KernelPCA(kernel='rbf', gamma=10)
X_kpca = kpca.fit_transform(X)
plt.figure()
plt.subplot(2, 2, 1, aspect='equal')
plt.title("Original space")
reds = y == 0
blues = y == 1
plt.plot(X[reds, 0], X[reds, 1], "ro")
plt.plot(X[blues, 0], X[blues, 1], "bo")
plt.xlabel("$x_1$")
plt.ylabel("$x_2$")
plt.subplot(2, 2, 3, aspect='equal')
plt.plot(X_kpca[reds, 0], X_kpca[reds, 1], "ro")
```

```
plt.plot(X_kpca[blues, 0], X_kpca[blues, 1], "bo")
plt.title("Projection by KPCA")
plt.xlabel("1st principal component in space induced by $\phi$")
plt.ylabel("2nd component")
plt.subplots_adjust(0.02, 0.10, 0.98, 0.94, 0.04, 0.35)
plt.show()
#print('gamma= %0.2f' %gamma)
```

As we have seen, a major obstacle to the success of a supervised learning algorithm is the translation from training data to test data. A labeled training set may have distinctive characteristics that are not present in new unlabeled data. We have seen that we can train our model to be quite precise on training data, yet this precision may not be translated to our unlabeled test data. Overfitting is an important problem in supervised learning and there are many techniques you can use to minimize it. A way to evaluate the estimator performance of the model on a training set is to use cross validation. Let's try this out on our iris data using a support vector machine. The first thing that we need to do is split our data into training and test sets. The `train_test_split` method takes two data structures: the data itself and the target. They can be either NumPy arrays, Pandas DataFrames lists, or SciPy matrices. As you would expect, the target needs to be the same length as the data. The `test_size` argument can either be a float between 0 and 1, representing the proportion of data included in the split, or an int representing the number of test samples. Here, we have used a `test_size` object as .3, indicating that we are holding out 40% of our data for testing.

In this example, we use the `svm.SVC` class and the `.score` method to return the mean accuracy of the test data in predicting the labels:

```
from sklearn.cross_validation import train_test_split
from sklearn import datasets
from sklearn import svm
from sklearn import cross_validation
iris = datasets.load_iris()
X_train, X_test, y_train, y_test = train_test_split (iris.data,
iris.target, test_size=0.4, random_state=0)
clf = svm.SVC(kernel='linear', C=1).fit(X_train, y_train)
scores=cross_validation.cross_val_score(clf, X_train, y_train, cv=5)
print("Accuracy: %0.2f (+/- %0.2f)" % (scores.mean(), scores.std() * 2))
```

You will observe the following output:

```
Accuracy: 0.99 (+/- 0.05)
```

Support vector machines have a `penalty` parameter that has to be set manually, and it is quite likely that we will run the SVC many times and adjust this parameter until we get an optimal fit. Doing this, however, leaks information from the training set to the test set, so we may still have the problem of over fitting. This is a problem for any estimator that has parameters that must be set manually, and we will explore this further in *Chapter 4*, *Models – Learning from Information*.

Summary

We have seen a basic kit of machine learning tools and a few indications of their uses on simple datasets. What you may be beginning to wonder is how these tools can be applied to real-world problems. There is considerable overlap between each of the libraries we have discussed. Many perform the same task, but add or perform the same function in a different way. Choosing which library to use for each problem is not necessarily a definitive decision. There is no best library; there is only the preferred library, and this varies from person to person, and of course, to the specifics of the application.

In the next chapter, we will look at one of the most important, and often overlooked, aspects of machine learning, that is, data.

3
Turning Data into Information

Raw data can be in many different formats and of varying quantity and quality. Sometimes, we are overwhelmed with data, and sometimes we struggle to get every last drop of information from our data. For data to become information, it requires some meaningful structure. We often have to deal with incompatible formats, inconsistencies, errors, and missing data. It is important to be able to access different parts of the dataset or extract subsets of the data based on some relational criteria. We need to spot patterns in our data and get a feel for how the data is distributed. We can use many tools to find this information hidden in data from visualizations, running algorithms, or just looking at the data in a spreadsheet.

In this chapter, we are going to introduce the following broad topics:

- Big data
- Data properties
- Data sources
- Data processing and analysis

But first, let's take a look into the following explanations:

What is data?

Data can be stored on a hard drive, streamed through a network, or captured live through sensors such as video cameras and microphones. If we are sampling from physical phenomena, such as a video or sound recording, the space is continuous and effectively infinite. Once this space is sampled, that is digitalized, a finite subset of this space has been created and at least some minimal structure has been imposed on it. The data is on a hard drive, encoded in bits, given some attributes such as a name, creation date, and so on. Beyond this, if the data is to be made use of in an application, we need to ask, "how is the data organized and what kinds of queries does it efficiently support?"

When faced with an unseen dataset, the first phase is exploration. Data exploration involves examining the components and structure of data. How many samples does it contain, and how many dimensions are in each sample? What are the data types of each dimension? We should also get a feel for the relationships between variables and how they are distributed. We need to check whether the data values are in line with what we expect. Are there are any obvious errors or gaps in the data?

Data exploration must be framed within the scope of a particular problem. Obviously, the first thing to find out is if it is likely that the dataset will provide useful answers. Is it worth our while to continue, or do we need to collect more data? Exploratory data analysis is not necessarily carried out with a particular hypothesis in mind, but perhaps with a sense of which hypotheses are likely to provide useful information.

Data is evidence that can either support or disprove a hypothesis. This evidence is only meaningful if it can be compared to a competing hypothesis. In any scientific process, we use a control. To test a hypothesis, we need to compare it to an equivalent system where the set of variables we are interested in remain fixed. We should attempt to show causality with a mechanism and explanation. We need a plausible reason for our observations. We should also consider that the real world is composed of multiple interacting components, and dealing with multivariate data can lead to exponentially increasing complexity.

It is with these things in mind, a sketch of the territory we are seeking to explore, that we approach new datasets. We have an objective, a point we hope to get to, and our data is a map through this unknown terrain.

Big data

The amount of data that's being created and stored on a global level is almost inconceivable, and it just keeps growing. Big data is a term that describes the large volume of data — both structured and unstructured. Let's now delve deeper into big data, beginning with the challenges of big data.

Challenges of big data

Big data is characterized by three challenges. They are as follows:

- The volume of the data
- The velocity of the data
- The variety of the data

Data volume

The volume problem can be approached from three different directions: **efficiency**, **scalability**, and **parallelism**. Efficiency is about minimizing the time it takes for an algorithm to process a unit of information. A component of this is the underlying processing power of the hardware. The other component, and the one that we have more control over, is ensuring that our algorithms are not wasting precious processing cycles with unnecessary tasks.

Scalability is really about brute force and throwing as much hardware at a problem as you can. Taking into account **Moore's law**, which states that the trend of computer power doubling every two years, will continue until it reaches its limit; it is clear that scalability is not, by itself, going to be able to keep up with the ever-increasing amounts of data. Simply adding more memory and faster processors is not, in many cases, going to be a cost effective solution.

Parallelism is a growing area of machine learning, and it encompasses a number of different approaches, from harnessing the capabilities of multi-core processors, to large-scale distributed computing on many different platforms. Probably, the most common method is to simply run the same algorithm on many machines, each with a different set of parameters. Another method is to decompose a learning algorithm into an adaptive sequence of queries, and have these queries processed in parallel. A common implementation of this technique is known as **MapReduce**, or its open source version, **Hadoop**.

Data velocity

The velocity problem is often approached in terms of data producers and data consumers. The rate of data transfer between the two is called the velocity, and it can be measured in interactive response times. This is the time it takes from a query being made to its response being delivered. Response times are constrained by latencies, such as hard disk read and write times, and the time it takes to transmit data across a network.

Data is being produced at ever greater rates, and this is largely driven by the rapid expansion of mobile networks and devices. The increasing instrumentation of daily life is revolutionizing the way products and services are delivered. This increasing flow of data has led to the idea of **streaming processing**. When input data is at a velocity that makes it impossible to store in its entirety, a level of analysis is necessary as the data streams, in essence, deciding what data is useful and should be stored, and what data can be thrown away. An extreme example is the **Large Hadron Collider** at CERN, where the vast majority of data is discarded. A sophisticated algorithm must scan the data as it is being generated, looking at the information needle in the data haystack. Another instance that processing data streams may be important is when an application requires an immediate response. This is becoming increasingly used in applications such as online gaming and stock market trading.

It is not just the velocity of incoming data that we are interested in; in many applications, particularly on the web, the velocity of a systems output is also important. Consider applications such as recommender systems that need to process a large amount of data and present a response in the time it takes for a web page to load.

Data variety

Collecting data from different sources invariably means dealing with misaligned data structures and incompatible formats. It also often means dealing with different semantics and having to understand a data system that may have been built on a fairly different set of logical premises. We have to remember that, very often, data is repurposed for an entirely different application from the one it was originally intended for. There is a huge variety of data formats and underlying platforms. Significant time can be spent converting data into one consistent format. Even when this is done, the data itself needs to be aligned such that each record consists of the same number of features and is measured in the same units.

Consider the relatively simple task of harvesting data from web pages. The data is already structured through the use of a mark language, typically HTML or XML, and this can help give us some initial structure. Yet, we just have to peruse the web to see that there is no standard way of presenting and tagging content in an information-relevant way. The aim of XML is to include content-relevant information in markup tags, for instance, by using tags for *author* or *subject*. However, the usage of such tags is far from universal and consistent. Furthermore, the web is a dynamic environment and many web sites go through frequent structural changes. These changes will often break web applications that expect a specific page structure.

The following diagram shows two dimensions of the big data challenge. I have included a few examples where these domains might approximately sit in this space. Astronomy, for example, has very few sources. It has a relatively small number of telescopes and observatories. Yet the volume of data that astronomers deal with is huge. On the other hand, perhaps, let's compare it to something like environmental sciences, where the data comes from a variety of sources, such as remote sensors, field surveys, validated secondary materials, and so on.

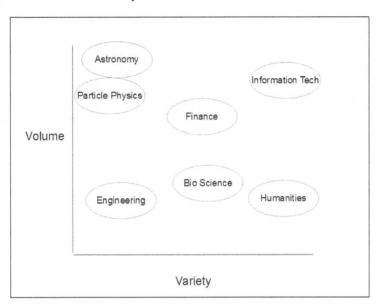

Integrating different data sets can take a significant amount of development time; up to 90 percent in some cases. Each project's data requirements will be different, and an important part of the design process is positioning our data sets with regard to these three elements.

Data models

A fundamental question for the data scientist is how the data is stored. We can talk about the hardware, and in this respect, we mean nonvolatile memory such as the hard drive of a computer or flash disk. Another way of interpreting the question (a more logical way) is how is the data organized? In a personal computer, the most visible way that data is stored is hierarchically, in nested folders and files. Data can also be stored in a table format or in a spreadsheet. When we are thinking about structure, we are interested in categories and category types, and how they are related. In a table, how many columns do we need, and in a relational data base, how are tables linked? A data model should not try to impose a structure on the data, but rather find a structure that most naturally emerges from the data.

Data models consist of three components:

- **Structure**: A table is organized into columns and rows; tree structures have nodes and edges, and dictionaries have the structure of key value pairs.

- **Constraints**: This defines the type of valid structures. For a table, this would include the fact that all rows have the same number of columns, and each column contains the same data type for every row. For example, a column, `items sold`, would only contain integer values. For hierarchical structures, a constraint would be a folder that can only have one immediate parent.

- **Operations**: This includes actions such as finding a particular value, given a key, or finding all rows where the items sold are greater than 100. This is sometimes considered separate from the data model because it is often a higher-level software layer. However, all three of these components are tightly coupled, so it makes sense to think of the operations as part of the data model.

To encapsulate raw data with a data model, we create databases. Databases solve some key problems:

- **They allow us to share data**: It gives multiple users access to the same data with varying read and write privileges.

- **They enforce a data model**: This includes not only the constraints imposed by the structure, say parent child relationships in a hierarchy, but also higher-level constraints such as only allowing one user named *bob*, or being a number between one and eight.

- **They allow us to scale**: Once the data is larger than the allocated size of our volatile memory, mechanisms are needed to both facilitate the transfer of data and also allow the efficient traversal of a large number of rows and columns.

- **Databases allow flexibility**: They essentially try to hide complexity and provide a standard way of interacting with data.

Data distributions

A key characteristic of data is its probability distribution. The most familiar distribution is the normal or Gaussian distribution. This distribution is found in many (all?) physical systems, and it underlies any random process. The normal function can be defined in terms of a **probability density function**:

$$f(x) = \frac{1}{\left(\sigma\sqrt{2\pi}\right)} \frac{e^{-(x-\mu)^2}}{\left(2\sigma^2\right)}$$

Here, δ (**sigma**) is the **standard deviation** and μ (**mu**) is the **mean**. This equation simply describes the relative likelihood a random variable, **x**, will take on a given value. We can interpret the standard deviation as the width of a bell curve, and the mean as its center. Sometimes, the term **variance** is used, and this is simply the square of the standard deviation. The standard deviation essentially measures how spread out the values are. As a general rule of thumb, in a normal distribution, 68% of the values are within 1 standard deviation of the mean, 95% of values are within 2 standard deviations of the mean, and 99.7% are within 3 standard deviations of the mean.

We can get a feel for what these terms do by running the following code and calling the `normal()` function with different values for the mean and variance. In this example, we create the plot of a normal distribution, with a mean of 1 and a variance of 0.5:

```
import numpy as np
import matplotlib.pyplot as plt
import matplotlib.mlab as mlab


def normal(mean = 0, var = 1):
    sigma = np.sqrt(var)
    x = np.linspace(-3,3,100)
    plt.plot(x,mlab.normpdf(x,mean,sigma))
    plt.show()


normal(1,0.5)
```

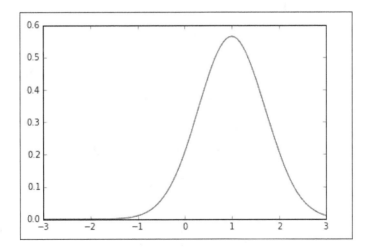

Related to the Gaussian distribution is the binomial distribution. We actually obtain a normal distribution by repeating a binomial process, such as tossing a coin. Over time, the probability approaches that half the tosses will result in heads.

$$P(x) = \frac{(n!)}{(x!(n-x)!)} p^{(x)} q^{(n-x)}$$

In this formula, **n** is the number coin tosses, **p** is the probability that half the tosses are heads, and **q** is the probability (*1-p*) that half the tosses are tails. In a typical experiment, say to determine the probability of various outcomes of a series of coin tosses, **n**, we can perform this many times, and obviously the more times we perform the experiment, the better our understanding of the statistical behavior of the system:

```
from scipy.stats import binom
def binomial(x=10,n=10, p=0.5):
    fig, ax = plt.subplots(1, 1)
    x=range(x)
    rv = binom(n, p)
    plt.vlines(x, 0, (rv.pmf(x)), colors='k', linestyles='-')
    plt.show()
binomial()
```

You will observe the following output:

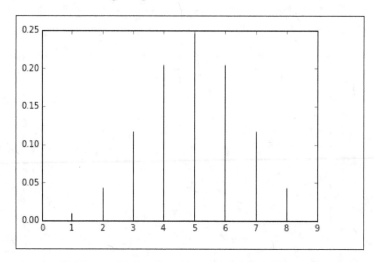

Another aspect of discrete distributions is understanding the likelihood of a given number of events occurring within a particular space and/or time. If we know that a given event occurs at an average rate, and each event occurs independently, we can describe it as a Poisson distribution. We can best understand this distribution using a probability mass function. This measures the probability of a given event that will occur at a given point in space/time.

The Poisson distribution has two parameters associated with it: **lambda** ,λ, a real number greater than 0, and k, an integer that is 0, 1, 2, and so on.

$$f(k;\lambda) = \Pr(X = k) = \lambda^k \frac{e^\lambda}{k}!$$

Here, we generate the plot of a Poisson distribution using the `scipy.stats` module:

```
from scipy.stats import poisson
def pois(x=1000):
    xr=range(x)
    ps=poisson(xr)
    plt.plot(ps.pmf(x/2))
pois()
```

The output of the preceding commands is as shown in the following diagram:

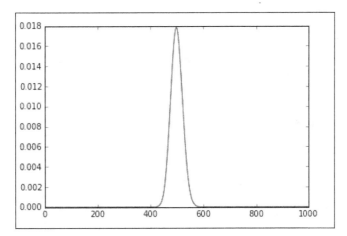

We can describe continuous data distributions using probability density functions. This describes the likelihood that a continuous random variable will take on a specified value. For univariate distributions, that is, those where there is only one random variable, the probability of finding a point X on an interval (a,b) is given by the following:

$$\int_{a}^{b} f_X(x)\,dx$$

This describes the fraction of a sampled population for which a value, **x**, lies between **a** and **b**. Density functions really only have meaning when they are integrated, and this will tell us how densely a population is distributed around certain values. Intuitively, we understand this as the area under the graph of its probability function between these two points. The **Cumulative Density Function (CDF)** is defined as the integral of its probability density functions, **fx**:

$$F_{\gamma}(x)^{-} \int_{-m}^{x} f_X(u)\,du$$

The CDF describes the proportion of a sampled population having values for a particular variable that is less than **x**. The following code shows a discrete (binomial) cumulative distribution function. The **s1** and **s2** shape parameters determine the step size:

```
import scipy.stats as stats
def cdf(s1=50,s2=0.2):

    x = np.linspace(0,s2 * 100,s1 *2)
    cd = stats.binom.cdf
    plt.plot(x,cd(x, s1, s2))
    plt.show()
```

Data from databases

We generally interact with databases via a query language. One of the most popular query languages is MySQL. Python has a database specification, PEP 0249, which creates a consistent way to work with numerous database types. This makes the code we write more portable across databases and allows a richer span of database connectivity. To illustrate how simple this is, we are going to use the `mysql.connector` class as an example. MySQL is one of the most popular database formats, with a straight forward, human-readable query language. To practice using this class, you will need to have a MySQL server installed on your machine. This is available from `https://dev.mysql.com/downloads/mysql/`.

This should also come with a test database called **world**, which includes statistical data on world cities.

Ensure that the MySQL server is running, and run the following code:

```
import mysql.connector
from mysql.connector import errorcode


cnx = mysql.connector.connect(user='root', password='password',
                                database='world', buffered=True)
cursor=cnx.cursor(buffered=True)
query=("select * from city where population > 1000000 order by
population")
cursor.execute(query)
worldList=[]
for (city) in cursor:
    worldList.append([city[1],city[4]])
cursor.close()
cnx.close()
```

Data from the Web

Information on the web is structured into HTML or XML documents. Markup tags give us clear *hooks* for us to sample our data. Numeric data will often appear in a table, and this makes it relatively easy to use because it is already structured in a meaningful way. Let's look at a typical excerpt from an HTML document:

```
<table border="0" cellpadding="5" cellspacing="2" class="details"
width="95%">
```

```
    <tbody>

    <th>Species</th>
    <th>Data1</th>
    <th>data2</th>
    </tr>

    <td>whitefly</td>
    <td>24</td>
    <td>76</td>
    </tr>
    </tbody>
  </table>
```

This shows the first two rows of a table, with a heading and one row of data containing two values. Python has an excellent library, Beautiful Soup, for extracting data from HTML and XML documents. Here, we read some test data into an array, and put it into a format that would be suitable for input in a machine learning algorithm, say a linear classifier:

```python
import urllib
from bs4 import BeautifulSoup
import numpy as np


url = urllib.request.urlopen
("http://interthing.org/dmls/species.html");
html = url.read()
soup = BeautifulSoup(html, "lxml")
table = soup.find("table")


headings = [th.get_text() for th in table.find("tr").find_all("th")]


datasets = []
for row in table.find_all("tr")[1:]:
    dataset = list(zip(headings, (td.get_text() for td in row.find_
all("td"))))
    datasets.append(dataset)


nd=np.array(datasets)
```

```
features=nd[:,1:,1].astype('float')
targets=(nd[:,0,1:]).astype('str')
print(features)
print(targets)
```

As we can see, this is relatively straight forward. What we need to be aware of is that we are relying on our source web page to remain unchanged, at least in terms of its overall structure. One of the major difficulties with harvesting data off the web in this way is that if the owners of the site decide to change the layout of their page, it will likely break our code.

Another data format you are likely to come across is the JSON format. Originally used for serializing Javascript objects, JSON is not, however, dependent on JavaScript. It is merely an encoding format. JSON is useful because it can represent hierarchical and multivariate data structures. It is basically a collection of key value pairs:

```
{"Languages":[{"Language":"Python","Version":"0"},{"Language":
"PHP","Version":"5"}],
"OS":{"Microsoft":"Windows 10", "Linux":"Ubuntu 14"},
"Name":"John\"the fictional\" Doe",
"location":{"Street":"Some Street", "Suburb":"Some Suburb"},
"Languages":[{"Language":"Python","Version":"0"},{"Language":"PHP"
,"Version":"5"}]
}
```

If we save the preceding JSON to a file called `jsondata.json`:

```
import json
from pprint import pprint


with open('jsondata.json') as file:
    data = json.load(file)


pprint(data)
```

Data from natural language

Natural language processing is one of the more difficult things to do in machine learning because it is focuses on what machines, at the moment, are not very good at: understanding the structure in complex phenomena.

As a starting point, we can make a few statements about the problem space we are considering. The number of words in any language is usually very large compared to the subset of words that are used in a particular conversation. Our data is sparse compared to the space it exists in. Moreover, words tend to appear in predefined sequences. Certain words are more likely to appear together. Sentences have a certain structure. Different social settings, such as at work, home, or out socializing; or in formal settings such as communicating with regulatory authorities, government, and bureaucratic settings, all require the use overlapping subsets of a vocabulary. A part from cues such as body language, intonation eye contact, and so forth, the social setting is probably the most important factor when trying to extract meaning from *natural* language.

To work with natural language in Python, we can use the the **Natural Language Tool Kit** (**NLTK**). If it is not installed, you can execute the `pip install -U nltk` command.

The NLTK also comes with a large library of lexical resources. You will need to download these separately, and NLTK has a download manager accessible through the following code:

```
import nltk
nltk.download()
```

A window should open where you can browse through the various files. This includes a range of books and other written material, as well as various lexical models. To get started, you can just download the package, `Book`.

A text corpus is a large body of text consisting of numerous individual text files. NLTK comes with **corpora** from a variety of sources such as classical literature (the Gutenberg Corpus), the web and chat text, Reuter news, and corpus containing text categorized by genres such as new, editorial, religion, fiction, and so on. You can also load any collection of text files using the following code:

```
from nltk.corpus import PlaintextCorpusReader
corpusRoot= 'path/to/corpus'
yourCorpus=PlaintextCorpusReader(corpusRoot, '.*')
```

The second argument to the `PlaintextCorpusReader` method is a regular expression indicating the files to include. Here, it simply indicates that all the files in that directory are included. This second parameter could also be a list of file locations, such as `['file1', 'dir2/file2']`.

Let's take a look at one of the existing corpora, and as an example, we are going to load the Brown corpus:

```
from nltk.corpus import brown
cat=brown.categories()
print(cat)


['adventure', 'belles_lettres', 'editorial', 'fiction', 'government',
'hobbies', 'humor', 'learned', 'lore', 'mystery', 'news', 'religion',
'reviews', 'romance', 'science_fiction']
```

The Brown corpus is useful because it enables us to study the systemic differences between genres. Here is an example:

```
from nltk.corpus import brown
cats=brown.categories()
for cat in cats:
    text=brown.words(categories=cat)
    fdist = nltk.FreqDist(w.lower() for w in text)
    posmod = ['love', 'happy', 'good', 'clean']
    negmod = ['hate', 'sad', 'bad', 'dirty']
    pcount=[]
    ncount=[]
    for m in posmod:
        pcount.append(fdist[m])
    for m in negmod:
        ncount.append(fdist[m])

    print(cat + ' positive: ' + str(sum(pcount)))
    print(cat + ' negative: ' + str(sum(ncount)))
    rat=sum(pcount)/sum(ncount)
    print('ratio= %s'%rat )
    print()
```

Here, we have sort of extracted sentiment data from different genres by comparing the occurrences of four positive sentiment words with their antonyms.

Data from images

Images are a rich and easily available source of data, and they are useful for learning applications such as object recognition, grouping, grading objects, as well as image enhancement. Images, of course, can be put together as a time series. Animating images is useful for both presentation and analysis; for example, we can use video to study trajectories, monitor environments, and learn dynamic behavior.

Image data is structured as a grid or matrix with color values assigned to each pixel. We can get a feel of how this works by using the Python Image Library. For this example, you will need to execute the following lines:

```
from PIL import Image
from matplotlib import pyplot as plt
import numpy as np
image= np.array(Image.open('data/sampleImage.jpg'))
plt.imshow(image, interpolation='nearest')
plt.show()
print(image.shape)


Out[10]: (536, 800, 3)
```

We can see that this particular image is 536 pixels wide and 800 pixels high. There are 3 values per pixel, representing color values between 0 and 255, for red, green, and blue respectively. Note that the co-ordinate system's origin *(0,0)* is the top left corner. Once we have our images as NumPy arrays, we can start working with them in interesting ways, for example, taking slices:

```
im2=image[0:100,0:100,2]
```

Data from application programming interfaces

Many social networking platforms have Application programming interfaces (APIs) that give the programmer access to various features. These interfaces can generate quite large amounts of streaming data. Many of these APIs have variable support for Python 3 and some other operating systems, so be prepared to do some research regarding the compatibility of systems.

Gaining access to a platform's API usually involves registering an application with the vendor and then using supplied security credentials, such as public and private keys, to authenticate your application.

Let's take a look at the Twitter API, which is relatively easy to access and has a well-developed library for Python. To get started, we need to load the Twitter library. If you do not have it already, simply execute the `pip install twitter` command from your Python command prompt.

You will need a Twitter account. Sign in and go to apps.twitter.com. Click on the **Create New App** button and fill out the details on the **Create An Application** page. Once you have submitted this, you can access your credential information by clicking on your app from the application management page and then clicking on the **Keys and Access Tokens** tab.

The four items we are interested in here are the API Key, the API Secret, The Access token, and the Access Token secret. Now, to create our `Twitter` object:

```
from twitter import Twitter, OAuth
#create our twitter object
t = Twitter(auth=OAuth(accesToken, secretToken, apiKey, apiSecret))

#get our home time line
home=t.statuses.home_timeline()

#get a public timeline
anyone= t.statuses.user_timeline(screen_name="abc730")

#search for a hash tag
pycon=t.search.tweets(q="#pycon")

#The screen name of the user who wrote the first 'tweet'
user=anyone[0]['user']['screen_name']

#time tweet was created
created=anyone[0]['created_at']

#the text of the tweet
text= anyone[0]['text']
```

You will, of course, need to fill in the authorization credentials that you obtained from Twitter earlier. Remember that in a publicly accessible application, you never have these credentials in a human-readable form, and certainly not in the file itself, and preferably encrypted outside a public directory.

Signals

A form of data that is often encountered in primary scientific research is various binary streams. There are specific codecs for video and audio transmission and storage, and often, we are looking for higher-level tools to deal with each specific format. There are various signal sources we might be considering such as from a radio telescopes, sensor on a camera, or the electrical impulses from a microphone. Signals all share the same underlying principles based on wave mechanics and harmonic motion.

Signals are generally studied using time frequency analysis. The central concept here is that a continuous signal in time and space can be decomposed into frequency components. We use what is known as a **Fourier Transform** to move between the time and frequency domains. This utilizes the interesting fact that states that any given function, including non periodic functions, can be represented by a series of sine and cosine functions. This is illustrated by the following:

$$F(x) = \frac{a_0}{2} + \sum_{n=1}^{m} (a_n cosnx + b_n sinnx)$$

To make this useful, we need to find the values for a_n and b_n. We do this by multiplying both sides of the equation cosine, mx, and integrating. Here m is an integer.

$$\int_{-\pi}^{\pi} f(x) cosmx \, dx = \frac{a_0}{2} \int_{-\pi}^{\pi} cosmx \, dx + \sum a_n \int_{-\pi}^{\pi} cosnx \, cosmx \, dx + b_n \int_{-\pi}^{\pi} \sin nx \, cosmx \, dx$$

This is called an **orthogonal function,** in a similar notion to how we consider x, y, and z to be orthogonal in a vector space. Now, if you can remember all your trigonometric functions, you will know that *sine* times *cosine* with integer coefficients is always zero between negative *pi* and *pi*. If we do the calculation, it turns out that the middle term on the left-hand side is zero, except when n equals m. In this case, the term equals *pi*. Knowing this, we can write the following:

$$a_n = \Pi \int_{-\Pi}^{\Pi} f(x) \cos nx \, dx$$

So, in the first step, if we multiply by *sin mx* instead of *cosine mx*, then we can derive the value of b_n.

$$b_n = \Pi^1 \int_{-\Pi}^{\Pi} f(x)\sin nx\, dx$$

We can see that we have decomposed a signal into a series of *sine* values and *cosine* values. This enables us to separate the frequency components of a signal.

Data from sound

One of the most common and easy to study signals is audio. We are going to use the soundfile module. You can install it via pip if you do not have it. The soundfile module has a wavfile.read class that returns the .wav file data as a NumPy array. To try the following code, you will need a short 16 bit wave file called audioSamp.wav. This can be downloaded from davejulian.net/mlbook. Save it in your data directory, in your working directory:

```
import soundfile as sf
import matplotlib.pyplot as plt
import numpy as np


sig, samplerate = sf.read('data/audioSamp.wav')
sig.shape
```

We see that the sound file is represented by a number of samples, each with two values. This is effectively the function as a vector, which describes the .wav file. We can, of course, create slices of our sound file:

```
slice=sig[0:500,:]
```

Here, we slice the first 500 samples. Let's calculate the Fourier transform of the slice and plot it:

```
ft=np.abs(np.fft.fft(slice))
Finally lets plot the result
plt.plot(ft)
plt.plot(slice)
```

The output of the preceding commands is as follows:

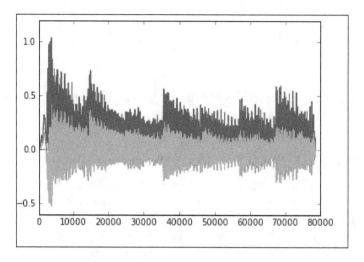

Cleaning data

To gain an understanding of which cleaning operations may be required for a particular dataset, we need to consider how the data was collected. One of the major cleaning operations involves dealing with missing data. We have already encountered an example of this in the last chapter, when we examined the temperature data. In this instance, the data had a quality parameter, so we could simply exclude the incomplete data. However, this may not be the best solution for many applications. It may be necessary to fill in the missing data. How do we decide what data to use? In the case of our temperature data, we could fill the missing values in with the average values for that time of year. Notice that we presuppose some domain knowledge, for example, the data is more or less periodic; it is in line with the seasonal cycle. So, it is a fair assumption that we could take the average for that particular date for every year we have a reliable record. However, consider that we are attempting to find a signal representing an increase in temperature due to climate change. In that case, taking the average for all years would distort the data and potentially hide a signal that could indicate warming. Once again, this requires extra knowledge and is specific about what we actually want to learn from the data.

Another consideration is that missing data may be one of three types, which are as follows:

- `empty`
- `zero`
- `null`

Different programming environments may treat these slightly differently. Out of the three, only zero is a measurable quantity. We know that zero can be placed on a number line before 1, 2, 3, and so on, and we can compare other numbers to zero. So, normally zero is encoded as numeric data. Empties are not necessarily numeric, and despite being empty, they may convey information. For example, if there is a field for *middle name* in a form, and the person filling out the form does not have a *middle name*, then an `empty` field accurately represents a particular situation, that is, having no middle name. Once again, this depends on the domain. In our temperature data, an `empty` field indicates missing data as it does not make sense for a particular day to have no maximum temperature. Null values, on the other hand, in computing, mean something slightly different from its everyday usage. For the computer scientist, null is not the same thing as no value or zero. Null values cannot be compared to anything else; they indicate that a field has a legitimate reason for not having an entry. Nulls are different than empty values. In our middle name example, a null value would indicate that it is unknown if the person has a middle name or not.

Another common data cleaning task is converting the data to a particular format. For our purposes here, the end data format we are interested in is a Python data structure such as a NumPy array. We have already looked at converting data from the JSON and HTML formats, and this is fairly straight forward.

Another format that we are likely to come across is the Acrobats **Portable Document Format (PDF)**. Importing data from PDF files can be quite difficult because PDF files are built on page layout primitives, and unlike HTML or JSON, they do not have meaningful markup tags. There are several non-Python tools for turning PDFs into text such as **pdftotext**. This is a command line tool that is included in many Linux distributions and is also available for Windows. Once we have converted the PDF file into text, we still need to extract the data, and the data embedded in the document determines how we can extract it. If the data is separated from the rest of the document, say in a table, then we can use Python's text parsing tools to extract it. Alternatively, we can use a Python library for working with PDF documents such as **pdfminer3k**.

Another common cleaning task is converting between data types. There is always the risk of losing data when converting between types. This happens when the target type stores less data than the source, for instance, converting to float 16 from float 32. Sometimes, we need to convert data at the file level. This occurs when a file has an implicit typing structure, for example, a spreadsheet. This is usually done within the application that created the file. For example, an Excel spreadsheet can be saved as a comma separated text file and then imported into a Python application.

Visualizing data

There are a number of reasons for why we visually represent the data. At the data exploration stage, we can gain an immediate understanding of data properties. Visual representation serves to highlight patterns in data and suggest modeling strategies. Exploratory graphs are usually made quickly and in large numbers. We are not so much concerned with aesthetic or stylistic issues, but we simply want to see what the data looks like.

Beyond using graphs to explore data, they are a primary means of communicating information about our data. Visual representation helps clarify data properties and stimulate viewer engagement. The human visual system is the highest bandwidth channel to the brain, and visualization is the most efficient way to present a large amount of information. By creating a visualization, we can immediately get a sense of important parameters, such as the maximum, minimum, and trends that may be present in the data. Of course, this information can be extracted from data through statistical analysis, however, analysis may not reveal specific patterns in the data that visualization will. The human visual pattern recognition system is, at the moment, significantly superior to that of a machine. Unless we have clues as to what we are looking for, algorithms may not pick out important patterns that a human visual system will.

The central problem for data visualization is mapping data elements to visual attributes. We do this by first classifying the data types as nominal, ordinal, or quantitative, and then determining which visual attributes represent each data type most effectively. Nominal or categorical data refers to a name, such as the species, male or female, and so on. Nominal data does not have a specific order or numeric value. Ordinal data has an intrinsic order, such as house numbers in a street, but is different from quantitative data in that it does not imply a mathematical interval. For example, it does not make much sense to multiply or divide house numbers. Quantitative data has a numeric value such as size or volume. Clearly, certain visual attributes are inappropriate for nominal data, such as size or position; they imply ordinal or quantitative information.

Sometimes, it is not immediately clear what each data type in a particular dataset is. One way to disambiguate this is to find what operations are applicable for each data type. For example, when we are comparing nominal data, we can use equals, for instance, the species **Whitefly** is not equal to the species **Thrip**. However, we cannot use operations such as greater than or less than. It does not make sense to say, in an ordinal sense, that one species is greater than another. With ordinal data, we can apply operations such as greater than or less than. Ordinal data has an implicit order that we can map on a number line. For quantitative data, this consists of an interval, such as a date range, to which we can apply additional operations such as subtractions. For example, we can not only say that a particular date occurs after another date, but we can also calculate the difference between the two dates. With quantitative data that has a fixed axis, that is a ratio of some fixed amount as opposed to an interval, we can use operations such as division. We can say that a particular object weighs twice as much or is twice as long as another object.

Once we are clear on our data types, we can start mapping them to attributes. Here, we will consider six visual attributes. They are position, size, texture, color, orientation, and shape. Of these, only position and size can accurately represent all three types of data. Texture, color, orientation, and shape, on the other hand, can only accurately represent nominal data. We cannot say that one shape or color is greater than another. However, we can associate a particular color or texture with a name.

Another thing to consider is the perceptual properties of these visual attributes. Research in psychology and psycho physics have established that visual attributes can be ranked in terms of how accurately they are perceived. Position is perceived most accurately, followed by length, angle, slope, area, volume, and finally, color and density, which are perceived with the least accuracy. It makes sense, therefore, to assign position and then length to the most important quantitative data. Finally, it should also be mentioned that we can encode, to some extent, ordinal data in a colors value (from dark to light) or continuous data in a color gradient. We cannot generally encode this data in a colors hue. For instance, there is no reason to perceive the color blue as somehow greater than the color red, unless you are making a reference to its frequency.

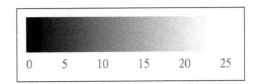

The color gradient to represent ordinal data

The next thing to consider is the number of dimensions that we need to display. For uni-variate data, that is, where we only need to display one variable, we have many choices such as dots, lines, or box plots. For bi-variate data, where we need to display two dimensions, the most common is with a scatter plot. For tri-variate data, it is possible to use a 3D plot, and this can be useful for plotting geometric functions such as manifolds. However, 3D plots have some drawbacks for many data types. It can be a problem to work out relative distances on a 3D plot. For instance, in the following figure, it is difficult to gauge the exact positions of each element. However, if we encode the z dimension as size, the relative values become more apparent:

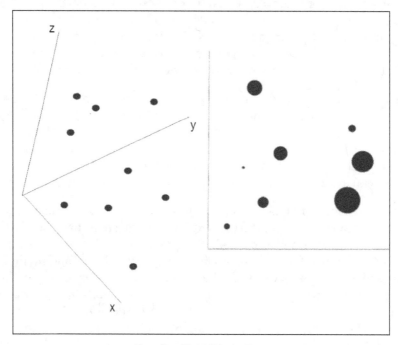

Encoding Three Dimensions

There is a large design space for encoding data into visual attributes. The challenge is to find the best mapping for our particular dataset and purpose. The starting point should be to encode the most important information in the most perceptually accurate way. Effective visual coding will depict all the data and not imply anything that is not in the data. For example, length implies quantitative data, so encoding non-quantitative data into length is incorrect. Another aspect to consider is consistency. We should choose attributes that make the most sense for each data type and use consistent and well-defined visual styles.

Summary

You have learned that there are a large number of data source, formats, and structures. You have hopefully gained some understanding of how to begin working with some of them. It is important to point out that in any machine learning project, working with the data at this fundamental level can comprise a significant proportion of the overall project development time.

In the next chapter, we will look at how we can put our data to work by exploring the most common machine learning models.

4
Models – Learning from Information

So far in this book, we have examined a range of tasks and techniques. We introduced the basics of data types, structures, and properties, and we familiarized ourselves with some of the machine learning tools that are available.

In this chapter, we will look at three broad types of model:

- Logical models
- Tree models
- Rule models

The next chapter will be devoted to another important type of model – the linear model. Much of the material in this chapter is theoretical, and its purpose is to introduce some of the mathematical and logical tools needed for machine learning tasks. I encourage you to work through these ideas and formulate them in ways that may help solve problems that we come across.

Logical models

Logical models divide the instance space, that is the set of all possible or allowable, instances, into segments. The goal is to ensure that the data in each segment is homogeneous with respect to a particular task. For example, if the task is classification, then we aim to ensure that each segment contains a majority of instances of the same class.

Logical models use logical expressions to explain a particular concept. The simplest and most general logical expressions are literals, and the most common of these is equality. The equality expression can be applied to all types—nominative, numerical, and ordinal. For numerical and ordinal types, we can include the inequality literals: greater than or less than. From here, we can build more complex expressions using four logical connectives. These are conjunction (logical AND), which is denoted by $\wedge$; disjunction (logical OR), which is denoted by $\vee$; implication, which is denoted by $\rightarrow$; and negation, which is denoted by $\neg$. This provides us with a way to express the following equivalences:

$$\neg \neg A \equiv A = A \rightarrow B \equiv \neg A \vee B$$

$$\neg (A \wedge B) \equiv \neg A \vee \neg B = \neg(A \vee B) \equiv \neg A \wedge \neg B$$

We can apply these ideas in a simple example. Let's say you come across a grove of trees that all appear to be from the same species. Our goal is to identify the defining features of this tree species for use in a classification task. For simplicity sake, let's say we are just dealing with the following four features:

- Size: This has three values—small, medium, and large
- Leaf type: This has two values—scaled or non-scaled
- Fruit: This has two values—yes or no
- Buttress: This has two values—yes or no

The first tree we identify can be described by the following conjunction:

Size = Large $\wedge$ Leaf = Scaled $\wedge$ Fruit = No $\wedge$ Buttress = Yes

The next tree that we come across is medium-sized. If we drop the size condition, then the statement becomes more general. That is, it will cover more samples:

Leaf = Scaled $\wedge$ Fruit = No $\wedge$ Buttress = Yes

The next tree is also medium-sized, but it does not have buttresses, so we remove this condition and generalize it to the following:

Leaf = Scaled $\wedge$ Fruit = No

The trees in the grove all satisfy this conjunction, and we conclude that they are conifers. Obviously, in a real-world example, we would use a greater range of features and values and employ more complex logical constructs. However, even in this simple example, the **instance space** is 3 2 2 2, which makes 24 possible instances. If we consider the absence of a feature as an additional value, then the **hypothesis space**, that is, the space that we can use to describe this set, is *4 3 3 3 = 108*. The number of sets of instances , or extensions, that are possible is 2^{24}. For example if you were to randomly choose a set of in. For example if you were to randomly choose a set of instances, the odds that you could find a conjunctive concept that exactly describes them is well over 100,000 to one.stances, the odds that you could find a conjunctive concept that exactly describes them is well over 100,000 to one.

Generality ordering

We can begin to map this hypothesis space from the most general statements to the most specific statements. For example, in the neighborhood of our conifer hypothesis, the space looks like this:

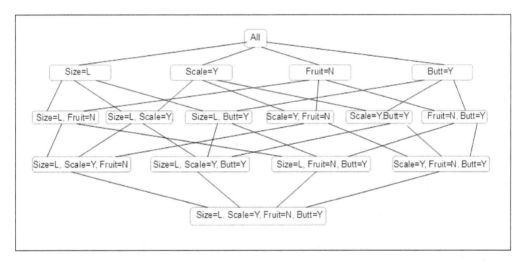

Here, we are ordering our hypothesis by generality. At the top is the most general hypothesis—all trees are conifers. The more general hypothesis will cover a greater number of instances, and therefore the most general hypothesis, that is, all trees are conifers, applies to all instances. Now, while this might apply to the grove we are standing in, when we attempt to apply this hypothesis to new data, that is, to trees outside the grove, it will fail. At the bottom of the preceding diagram, we have the least general hypothesis. As we make more observations and move up through the nodes, we can eliminate hypothesis and establish the next most general complete hypothesis. The most conservative generalization we can make from the data is called the **least general generalization (LGG)** of these instances. We can understand this as being the point in the hypothesis space where the paths upward from each of the instances intersect.

Let's describe our observations in a table:

Size	Scaled	Fruit	Buttress	Label
L	Y	N	Y	p1
M	Y	N	Y	p2
M	Y	N	N	p3
M	Y	N	Y	p4

Sooner or later, of course, you wander out of the grove and you observe negative examples—trees that are clearly not conifers. You note the following features;

Size	Scaled	Fruit	Buttress	Label
S	N	N	N	n1
M	N	N	N	n2
S	N	Y	N	n3
M	Y	N	N	n4

So, with the addition of the negative examples, we can still see that our least general complete hypothesis is still *Scale = Y ∧ Fruit =N*. However, you will notice that a negative example, *n4*, is covered. The hypothesis is therefore not consistent.

Version space

This simple example may lead you to the conclusion that there is only one LGG. But this is not necessarily true. We can expand our hypothesis space by adding a restricted form of disjunction called **internal disjunction**. In our previous example, we had three positive examples of conifers with either medium or large size. We can add a condition *Size = Medium ∨ Size = Large*, and we can write this as *size [m,l]*. Internal disjunction will only work with features that have more than two values because something like *Leaves = Scaled ∨ Leaves = Non-Scaled* is always `true`.

In the previous conifer example, we dropped the size condition to accommodate our second and third observations. This gave us the following LGG:

Leaf = Scaled ∧ Leaf = = No

Given our internal disjunction, we can rewrite the preceding LGG as follows:

Size[m,l] ∧ Leaf = Scaled ∧ Fruit = No

Now, consider the first non-conifer, or negative non-conifer example:

Size = Small ∧ Leaf =Non-scaled ∧ Fruit = No

We can drop any of the three conditions in the LGG with the internal disjunction without covering this negative example. However, when we attempt to generalize further to single conditions, we see that *Size[m,l]* and *Leaf = Scaled* are OK but *Fruit = No* is not, since it covers the negative example.

Now, we are interested in the hypothesis that is both **complete** and **consistent**, that is, it covers all the positive examples and none of the negative. Let's now redraw our diagram considering just our four positive (*p1 - p4*) examples and one negative example (*n1*).

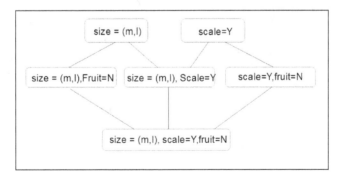

This is sometimes referred to as the **version space**. Note that we have one least general hypothesis, three intermediate, and, now, two most general hypotheses. The version space forms a convex set. This means we can interpolate between members of this set. If an element lies between a most general and least general member of the set, then it is also a member of that set. In this way, we can fully describe the version space by its most and least general members.

Consider a case where the least general generalization covers one or more of the negative instances. In such cases, we can say that the data is not **conjunctively separable** and the version space is empty. We can apply different approach whereby we search for the most general consistent hypothesis. Here we are interested in consistency as opposed to completeness. This essentially involves iterating through paths in the hypothesis space from the most general. We take downward steps by, for example, adding a conjunct or removing a value from an internal conjunct. At each step, we minimize the specialization of the resulting hypothesis.

Coverage space

When our data is not conjunctively separable, we need a way to optimize between consistency and completeness. A useful approach is in terms of mapping the **coverage space** of positive and negative instances, as shown in the following diagram:

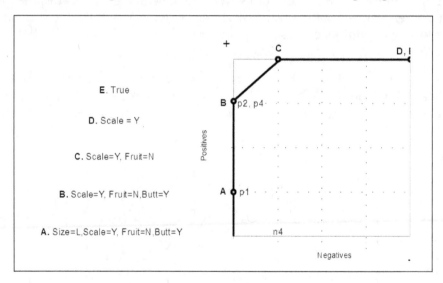

We can see that learning a hypothesis involves finding a path through the hypothesis space ordered by generality. Logical models involve finding a pathway through a latticed structured hypothesis space. Each hypothesis in this space covers a set of instances. Each of these sets has upper and lower bounds, in and are ordered by, generality. So far, we have only used single conjunctions of literals. With a rich logical language at our disposal, why not incorporate a variety of logical connectives into our expressions? There are basically two reasons why we may want to keep our expressions simple, as follows:

- More expressive statements lead to specialization, which will result in a model overfitting training data and performing poorly on test data
- Complicated descriptions are computationally more expensive than simple descriptions

As we saw when learning about the conjunctive hypothesis, uncovered positive examples allow us to drop literals from the conjunction, making it more general. On the other hand, covered negative examples require us to increase specialization by adding literals.

Rather than describing each hypothesis in terms of conjunctions of single literals, we can describe it in terms of disjunctions of clauses, where each clause can be of the form $A \rightarrow B$. Here, A is a conjunction of literals and B is a single literal. Let's consider the following statement that covers a negative example:

$Butt = Y \wedge Scaled = N \wedge Size = S \wedge \ulcorner Fruit = N$

To exclude this negative example, we can write the following clause:

$Butt = Y \wedge Scaled = N \wedge Size = S \rightarrow Fruit = N$

There are of course, other clauses that exclude the negative, such as $Butt = Y \rightarrow Fruit = N$; however, we are interested in the most specific clause because it is less likely to also exclude covered positives.

PAC learning and computational complexity

Given that, as we increase the complexity of our logical language, we impose a computational cost, we need a metric to gauge the *learnability* of a language. To these ends, we can use the idea of **Probably Approximately Correct** (PAC) learning.

When we select one hypothesis from a set of hypotheses, the goal is to ensure that our selection will have, with high probability, a low generalization error. This will perform with a high degree of accuracy on a test set. This introduces the idea of **computational complexity**. This is a formalization to gauge the computational cost of a given algorithm in relation to the accuracy of its output.

PAC learning makes allowance for mistakes on non-typical examples, and this typicality is determined by an unspecified probability distribution, D. We can evaluate an error rate of a hypothesis with respect to this distribution. For example, let's assume that our data is noise-free and that the learner always outputs a complete and consistent hypothesis within the training samples. Let's choose an arbitrary error rate $\epsilon < 0.5$ and a failure rate $\delta = 0.5$. We require our learning algorithm to output a hypothesis that has a probability $\geq 1 - \delta$ such that the error rate will be less than ϵ. It turns out that this will always be true for any reasonably sized training set. For example, if our hypothesis space, H, contains a single bad hypothesis, then the probability that it is complete and consistent on n independent training samples is less than or equal to $(1 - \epsilon)^n$. For any $0 \leq \epsilon \leq 1$, this probability is less than $e\text{-}n\ \epsilon$. We need to keep this below our error rate, δ, which we achieve by setting $n \geq 1/\epsilon\ ln\ 1/\delta$. Now, if H contains a number of bad hypotheses, $k \leq |\ H\ |$, then the probability that at least one of them is complete and consistent on n independent samples is at maximum:

$k(1 - \epsilon)n \leq |\ H\ |\ (1 - \epsilon)n \leq |\ H\ |\ e\text{-}n\ \epsilon$

This maximum will be less than f if the following condition is met:

$$n \leq \frac{1}{\epsilon}\left(\ln H + \ln \frac{1}{\delta} \right)$$

This is known as the **sample complexity** and you will notice that it is logarithmic in $1/\delta$ and linear in $1/\epsilon$.

 This implies that it is exponentially cheaper to reduce the failure rate than it is to reduce the error rate.

To conclude this section, I will make one further point. The hypothesis space H is a subset of U, a universe of explanation for any given phenomena. How do we know whether the correct hypothesis actually exists inside H rather than elsewhere in U? Bayes theorem shows a relationship between the relative probabilities of H and $\vdash H$ as well as their relative prior probabilities. However, there is no real way we can know the value of $P \vdash H$ because there is no way to calculate the probabilities of a hypothesis that has not yet been conceived. Moreover, the contents of this hypothesis consist of a, currently unknown, universe of possible objects. This paradox occurs in any description that uses comparative hypothesis checking where we evaluate our current hypothesis against other hypotheses within H. Another approach would be to find a way to evaluate H. We can see that, as we expand H, the computability of hypothesis within it becomes more difficult. To evaluate H, we need to restrict our universe to the universe of the known. For a human, this is a life of experiences that has been imprinted in our brains and nervous system; for a machine, it is the memory banks and algorithms. The ability to evaluate this global hypothesis space is one of the key challenges of artificial intelligence.

Tree models

Tree models are ubiquitous in machine learning. They are naturally suited to divide and conquer iterative algorithms. One of the main advantages of decision tree models is that they are naturally easy to visualize and conceptualize. They allow inspection and do not just give an answer. For example, if we have to predict a category, we can also expose the logical steps that give rise to a particular result. Also tree models generally require less data preparation than other models and can handle numerical and categorical data. On the down side, tree models can create overly complex models that do not generalize to new data very well. Another potential problem with tree models is that they can become very sensitive to changes in the input data and, as we will see later, this problem can be mitigated against using them as ensemble learners.

An important difference between decision trees and the hypothesis mapping used in the previous section is that the tree model does not use internal disjunction on features with more than two values but instead branches on each value. We can see this with the size feature in the following diagram:

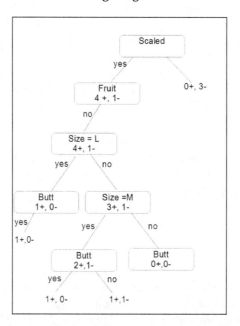

Another point to note is that decision trees are more expressive than the conjunctive hypothesis and we can see this here, where we have been able to separate the data where the conjunctive hypothesis covered negative examples. This expressiveness, of course, comes with a price: the tendency to overfit on training data. A way to force generalization and reduce overfitting is to introduce an inductive bias toward less complex hypotheses.

We can quite easily implement our little example using the Sklearn `DecisionTreeClassifier` and create an image of the resultant tree:

```
from sklearn import tree

names=['size','scale','fruit','butt']
labels=[1,1,1,1,1,0,0,0]

p1=[2,1,0,1]
p2=[1,1,0,1]
p3=[1,1,0,0]
p4=[1,1,0,0]
```

```
n1=[0,0,0,0]
n2=[1,0,0,0]
n3=[0,0,1,0]
n4=[1,1,0,0]
data=[p1,p2,p3,p4,n1,n2,n3,n4]

def pred(test, data=data):
    dtre=tree.DecisionTreeClassifier()
    dtre=dtre.fit(data,labels)
    print(dtre.predict([test]))
    with open('data/treeDemo.dot', 'w') as f:
        f=tree.export_graphviz(dtre,out_file=f,
                                feature_names=names)
pred([1,1,0,1])
```

Running the preceding code creates a `treeDemo.dot` file. The decision tree classifier, saved as a `.dot` file, can be converted into an image file such as a `.png`, `.jpeg` or `.gif` using the **Graphiz** graph visualization software. You can download Graphviz from `http://graphviz.org/Download.php`. Once you have it installed, use it to convert the `.dot` file into an image file format of your choice.

This gives you a clear picture of how the decision tree has been split.

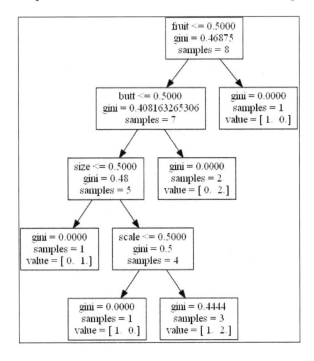

We can see from the full tree that we recursively split on each node, increasing the proportion of samples of the same class with each split. We continue down nodes until we reach a leaf node where we aim to have a homogeneous set of instances. This notion of purity is an important one because it determines how each node is split and it is behind the Gini values in the preceding diagram.

Purity

How do we understand the usefulness of each feature in relation to being able to split samples into classes that contain minimal or no samples from other classes? What are the indicative sets of features that give a class its label? To answer this, we need to consider the idea of purity of a split. For example, consider we have a set of Boolean instances, where D is split into $D1$ and $D2$. If we further restrict ourselves to just two classes, D^{pos} and D^{neg}, we can see that the optimum situation is where D is split perfectly into positive and negative examples. There are two possibilities for this: either where $D1^{pos} = D^{pos}$ and $D1^{neg} = \{\}$, or $D1^{neg} = D^{neg}$ and $D1^{pos} = \{\}$.

If this is true, then the children of the split are said to be pure. We can measure the impurity of a split by the relative magnitude of n^{pos} and n^{neg}. This is the empirical probability of a positive class and it can be defined by the proportion $p=n^{pos}/(n^{pos} + n^{neg})$. There are several requirements for an impurity function. First, if we switch the positive and negative class (that is, replace p with $1-p$) then the impurity should not change. Also the function should be zero when $p=0$ or $p=1$, and it should reach its maximum when $p=0.5$. In order to split each node in a meaningful way, we need an optimization function with these characteristics.

There are three functions that are typically used for impurity measures, or splitting criteria, with the following properties.

- **Minority class**: This is simply a measure of the proportion of misclassified examples assuming we label each leaf with the majority class. The higher this proportion is, the greater the number of errors and the greater the impurity of the split. This is sometimes called the **classification error**, and is calculated as $min(p,1-p)$.

- **Gini index**: This is the expected error if we label examples either positive, with probability p, or negative, with probability $1-p$. Sometimes, the square root of the Gini index is used as well, and this can have some advantages when dealing with highly skewed data where a large proportion of samples belongs to one class.

- **Entropy**: This measure of impurity is based on the expected information content of the split. Consider a message telling you about the class of a series of randomly drawn samples. The purer the set of samples, the more predictable this message becomes, and therefore the smaller the expected information. Entropy is measured by the following formula:

$$-plog_2 p - (1-p)\log_2(1-p)$$

These three splitting criteria, for a probability range of between *0* and *1*, are plotted in the following diagram. The entropy criteria are scaled by *0.5* to enable them to be compared to the other two. We can use the output from the decision tree to see where each node lies on this curve.

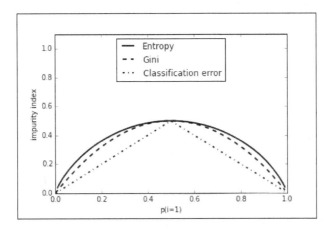

Rule models

We can best understand rule models using the principles of discrete mathematics. Let's review some of these principles.

Let *X* be a set of features, the feature space, and *C* be a set of classes. We can define the ideal classifier for *X* as follows:

c: *X* → *C*

A set of examples in the feature space with class *c* is defined as follows:

$D = \{(x_1, c(x_1)), \dots, (x_n, c(x_n)) \subseteq X \times C$

A splitting of X is partitioning X into a set of mutually exclusive subsets $X_1....X_s$, so we can say the following:

$X = X1 \cup .. \cup Xs$

This induces a splitting of D into $D_1,...D_s$. We define Dj where $j = 1,...,s$ and is $\{(x,c(x)) \in D \mid x \in Xj)\}$.

This is just defining a subset in X called Xj where all the members of Xj are perfectly classified.

In the following table we define a number of measurements using sums of indicator functions. An indicator function uses the notation where $I[...]$ is equal to one if the statement between the square brackets is true and zero if it is false. Here $\tau c(x)$ is the estimate of $c(x)$.

Let's take a look at the following table:

Number of positives	$P = \sum_{(x \in D)} I\left[c(x) = pos\right]$
Number of negatives	$N = \sum_{(x \in D)} I\left[c(x) = neg\right]$
True positives	$TP = \sum_{(x \in D)} I\left[\tau c(x) = c(x) = pos\right]$
True negatives	$TN = \sum_{(x \in D)} I\left[\tau c(x) = c(x) = neg\right]$
False positives	$FP = \sum_{(x \in D)} I\left[\tau c(x) = pos, c(x) = neg\right]$
False negatives	$FN = \sum_{(x \in D)} I\left[\tau(x) = neg, c(x) = pos\right]$
Accuracy	$acc = \dfrac{1}{D} \sum_{(x \in D)} I\left[\tau c(x) = c(x)\right]$
Error rate	$err = \dfrac{1}{D} \sum_{(x \in D)} I\left[\tau c(x) \neq c(x)\right]$
True positive rate (sensitivity, recall)	$tpr = \dfrac{\left(\sum_{(x \in D)} I\left[\tau c(x) = c(x) = pos\right]\right)}{\left(\sum_{(x \in D)} I\left[c(x) = pos\right]\right)} = \dfrac{TP}{P}$

True negative rate (negative recall)	$$tnr = \frac{\left(\sum_{(x \in D)} I\left[\tau c(x) = c(x) = neg\right]\right)}{\left(\sum_{(x \in D)} I\left[c(x) = neg\right]\right)} = \frac{TN}{N}$$
Precision, confidence	$$prec = \frac{\left(\sum_{(x \in D)} I\left[\tau c(x) = c(x) = pos\right]\right)}{\left(\sum_{(x \in D)} I\left[\tau c(x) = pos\right]\right)} = \frac{TP}{(TP + FP)}$$

Rule models comprise not only sets or lists of rules, but importantly, a specification on how to combine these rules to form predictions. They are a logical model but differ from the tree approach in that, trees split into mutually exclusive branches, whereas rules can overlap, possibly carrying additional information. In supervised learning there are essentially two approaches to rule models. One is to find a combination of literals, as we did previously, to form a hypothesis that covers a sufficiently homogeneous set of samples, and then find a label. Alternatively, we can do the opposite; that is, we can first select a class and then find rules that cover a sufficiently large subset of samples of that class. The first approach tends to lead to an ordered list of rules, and in the second approach, rules are an unordered set. Each deals with overlapping rules in its own characteristic way, as we will see. Let's look at the ordered list approach first.

The ordered list approach

As we add literals to a conjunctive rule, we aim to increase the homogeneity of each subsequent set of instances covered by the rule. This is similar to constructing a path in the hypothesis space as we did for our logical trees in the last section. A key difference with the rule approach is that we are only interested in the purity of one of the children, the one where the added literal is true. With tree-based models, we use the weighted average of both children to find the purity of both branches of a binary split. Here, we are still interested in calculating the purity of subsequent rules; however, we only follow one side of each split. We can still use the same methods for finding purity, but we no longer need to average over all children. As opposed to the divide and conquer strategy of decision trees, rule-based learning is often described as separate and conquer.

Let's briefly consider an example using our conifer categorization problem from the previous section.

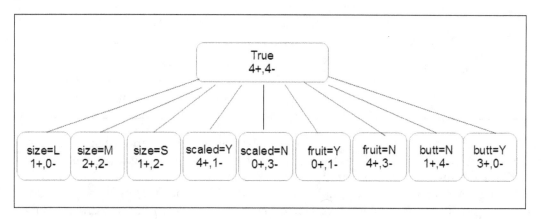

There are several options for choosing a rule that will result in the purest split. Supposing we choose the rule *If scaled = N then class is negative*, we have covered three out of four negative samples. In the next iteration, we remove these samples from consideration and continue this process of searching for literals with maximum purity. Effectively, what we are doing is building an ordered list of rules joined with the `if` and `else` clauses. We can rewrite our rules to be mutually exclusive, and this would mean that the set of rules does not need to be ordered. The tradeoff here is that we would have to use either negated literals or internal disjunctions to deal with features that have more than two values.

There are certain refinements we can make to this model. For example, we can introduce a stopping criterion that halts iteration if certain conditions are met, such as in the case of noisy data where we may want to stop iteration when the number of samples in each class falls below a certain number.

Ordered rule models have a lot in common with decision trees, especially, in that, they use an objective function based on the notion of purity that is the relative number of positive and negative class instances in each split. They have structures that are easy to visualize and they are used in many different machine learning settings.

Set-based rule models

With set based rule models rules are learned one class at a time, and our objective function simply becomes maximize p, rather than minimizing $\min(p,1-p)$. Algorithms that use this method typically iterate over each class and only cover samples of each class that are removed after a rule is found. Set-based models use precision (refer to table 4-1) as a search heuristic and this can make the model focus too much on the purity of the rule; it may miss near pure rules that can be further specialized to form a pure rule. Another approach, called **beam search**, uses a heuristic to order a predetermined number of best partial solutions.

Ordered lists give us a convex coverage for the training set. This is not necessarily true of the uncorded set-based approach where there is no global optimum order for a given set of rules. Because of this, we have access to rule overlaps expressed as a conjunction $A{\wedge}B$, where A and B are two rule sets. If these two rules are in an ordered list, we have either, if the order is AB, $A = (A{\wedge}B) \vee (A{\wedge} \ulcorner B)$ or, if the order is BA, $B = (A{\wedge}B) \vee (\ulcorner A{\wedge}B)$. This means that the rule space is potentially enlarged; however, because we have to estimate the coverage of overlaps, we sacrifice convexity.

Rule models, in general, are well suited to predictive models. We can, as we will see later, extend our rule models to perform such tasks as clustering and regression. Another important application of rule models is to build **descriptive models**. When we are building classification models, we generally look for rules that will create pure subsets of the training samples. However, this not necessarily true if we are looking for other distinguishing characteristics of a particular sample set. This is sometimes referred to as **subgroup discovery**. Here, we are not interested in a heuristic that is based on class purity but rather in one that looks for distinguishing class distributions. This is done using a defined quality function based on the idea of local exceptional testing. This function can take the form $q=TP/(FP+g)$. Here g is a generalization factor that determines the allowable number of nontarget class instances relative to the number of instances covered by the rule. For a small value of g, say less than *1*, rules will be generated that are more specific because every additional nontarget example incurs greater relative *expense*. Higher values of g, say greater than *10*, create more general rules covering more nontarget samples. There is no theoretical maximum value for g; however, it does not make much sense for it to exceed the number of samples. The value of g is governed by the size of the data and the proportion of positive samples. The value of g can be varied, thus guiding subgroup discovery to certain points in the TP versus FP space.

We can use subjective or objective quality functions. We can incorporate subjective *interestingness* coefficients into the model to reflect things such as understandability, unexpectedness, or, based on templates describing the interesting class, relationship patterns. Objective measurements are derived from the statistical and structural properties of the data itself. They are very amenable to the use of coverage plots to highlight subgroups that have statistical properties that differ from the population as a whole.

Finally, in this section on rule-based models, we will consider rules that can be learned entirely unsupervised. This is called **association rule learning**, and its typical use cases include data mining, recommender systems and natural language processing. We will use as an example a hardware shop that sells four items: **hammers**, **nails**, **screws**, and **paint**.

Let's take a look at the following table:

Transaction	Items
1	Nails
2	Hammers and nails
3	Hammers, nails, paint, and screws
4	Hammers, nails, and paint
5	Screws
6	Paint and screws
7	Screws and nails
8	Paint

In this table, we have grouped transactions with items. We could also have grouped each item with the transactions it was involved in. For example, nails were involved in transactions **1**, **2**, **3**, **4**, and **7**, and hammers were involved in **2**, **3**, **4**, and so on. We can also do this with sets of items, for example, **hammers** and **nails** were both involved in transactions **2**, **3**, and **4**. We can write this as the item set {hammer,nails} covers the transaction set [2,3,4]. There are 16 item sets including the empty set, which covers all transactions.

The relationship between transaction sets forms a lattice structure connecting items with their respective sets. In order to build associative rules, we need to create frequent item sets that exceed the threshold F_T. For example, a frequent item set where $F_T = 3$ is {screws}, {hammer,nails}, and {paint}. These are simply the items sets that are associated with three or more transactions. The following is a diagram showing part of the lattice from our example. In a similar way, we found the least general generalization in our hypothesis space mapping. Here, we are interested in the lowest boundary of the largest item set. In this example, it is {nails,hammer}.

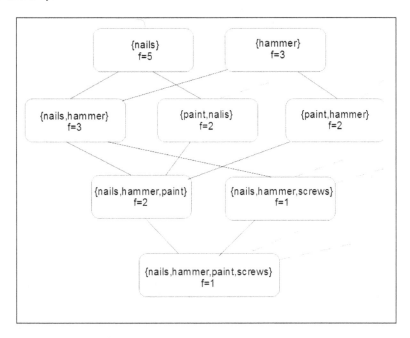

We can now create association rules of the form *if A then B*, where *A* and *B* are item sets that frequently appear together in a transaction. If we select an edge on this diagram, say the edge between {nails} with a frequency of 5, and {nails, hammer} with a frequency of 3, then we can say that the **confidence** of the association rule *if nails then hammer* is 3/5. Using a frequency threshold together with the confidence of a rule, an algorithm can find all rules that exceed this threshold. This is called **association rule mining**, and it often includes a post-processing phase where unnecessary rules are filtered out, for example—where a more specific rule does not have a higher confidence than a more general parent.

Summary

We began this chapter by exploring a logical language and creating a hypothesis space mapping for a simple example. We discussed the idea of least general generalizations and how to find a path through this space from the most general to the least general hypothesis. We briefly looked at the concept of *learnability*. Next, we looked at tree models and found that they can be applied to a wide range of tasks and are both descriptive and easy to interpret. Trees by themselves, however, are prone to overfitting and the greedy algorithms employed by most tree models can be prone to over-sensitivity to initial conditions. Finally, we discussed both ordered rule lists and unordered rule set-based models. The two different rule models are distinguished by how they handle rule overlaps. The ordered approach is to find a combination of literals that will separate the samples into more homogeneous groups. The unordered approach searches for a hypotheses one class at a time.

In the next chapter, we will look at quite a different type of model—the linear model. These models employ the mathematics of geometry to describe the problem space and, as we will see, form the basis for support vector machines and neural nets.

5
Linear Models

Linear models are one of the most widely used models and form the foundation of many advanced nonlinear techniques such as support vector machines and neural networks. They can be applied to any predictive task such as classification, regression, or probability estimation.

When responding to small changes in the input data, and provided that our data consists of entirely uncorrelated features, linear models tend to be more stable than tree models. As we mentioned in the last chapter, tree models can over-respond to small variations in training data. This is because splits at the root of a tree have consequences that are not recoverable further down the line, that is, producing different branching and potentially making the rest of the tree significantly different. Linear models on the other hand are relatively stable, being less sensitive to initial conditions. However, as you would expect, this has the opposite effect, changing less sensitive data to nuanced data. This is described by the terms **variance** (for over fitting models) and **bias** (for under fitting models). A linear model is typically low-variance and high-bias.

Linear models are generally best approached from a geometric perspective. We know we can easily plot two dimensions of space in a Cartesian co-ordinate system, and we can use the illusion of perspective to illustrate a third. We have also been taught to think of time as being a fourth dimension, but when we start speaking of n dimensions, a physical analogy breaks down. Intriguingly, we can still use many of the mathematical tools that we intuitively apply to three dimensions of space. While it becomes difficult to visualize these extra dimensions, we can still use the same geometric concepts, such as lines, planes, angles, and distance, to describe them. With geometric models, we describe each instance as having a set of real-value features, each of which is a dimension in our geometric space. Let's begin this chapter with a review of the formalism associated with linear models.

We have already disused the basic numerical linear model solution by the least squared method for two variables. It is straightforward and easy to visualize on a 2D coordinate system. When we try to add parameters, as we add features to our model, we need a formalism to replace, or augment, an intuitive visual representation. In this chapter, we will be looking at the following topics:

- The least squares method
- The normal equation method
- Logistic regression
- Regularization

Let's start with the basic model.

Introducing least squares

In a simple one-feature model, our hypothesis function is as follows:

$$h(x) = w_0 + w_1 x$$

If we graph this, we can see that it is a straight line crossing the y axis at w_0 and having a slope of w_1. The aim of a linear model is to find the parameter values that will create a straight line that most closely matches the data. We call these the functions parameter values. We define an objective function, J_w, which we want to minimize:

$$min J_w = \frac{1}{2m} \sum_{i=1}^{m} \left(h_w \left(x^{(i)} \right) - y^{(i)} \right)^2$$

Here, m is the number of training samples, $h_w(x^{(i)})$ is the estimated value of the ith training sample, and y^i is its actual value. This is the **cost function** of h, because it measures the cost of the error; the greater the error, the higher the cost. This method of deriving the cost function is sometime referred to as the **sum of the squared error** because it sums up the difference between the predicted value and the actual value. This sum is halved as a convenience, as we will see. There are actually two ways that we can solve this. We can either use an iterative gradient descent algorithm or minimize the cost function in one step using the normal equation. We will look at the gradient descent first.

Gradient descent

When we graph parameter values against the cost function, we get a bowl shaped convex function. As parameter values diverge from their optimized values in either direction (from a single minima), the cost of our model grows. As the hypothesis function is linear, the cost function is convex. If this was not the case, then it would be unable to distinguish between **global** and **local minimum**.

The gradient descent algorithm is expressed by the following update rule:

$$repeat\ until\ converges\ w_j := w_j - \alpha \frac{\delta}{(\delta w_j)} J_w$$

Where δ is the first derivative of J_w as it uses the sign of the derivative to determine which way to step. This is simply the sign of the slope of the tangent at each point. The algorithm takes a hyper parameter, a, which is the learning rate that we need to set. It is called a **hyper parameter** to distinguish it from the w parameters that are estimated by our model. If we set the learning rate too small, it will take longer to find the minimum; if set too high, it will overshoot. We may find that we need to run the model several times to determine the best learning rate.

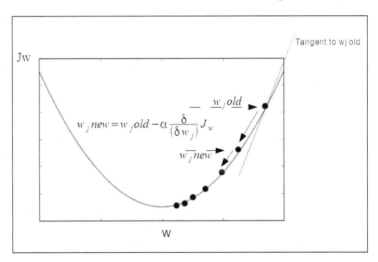

When we apply gradient descent to linear regression, the following formulas, which are the parameters of our model, can be derived. We can rewrite the derivative term to make it easier to calculate. The derivations themselves are quite complex, and it is unnecessary to work through them here. If you know calculus, you will be able to see that the following rules are equivalent. Here, we repeatedly apply two update rules to the hypothesis, employing a stopping function. This is usually when the differences between the parameters on subsequent iterations drop below a threshold, that is, t.

Initialize w_0 and w_1 and repeat:

$$\|wold - wnew\| < t\{$$

$$w_0 : w_0 - a\frac{1}{m}\sum_{i=1}^{m}\left(h_w\left(x^{(i)}\right) - y^{(i)}\right)$$

$$w_1 : w_0 - a\frac{1}{m}\sum_{i=1}^{m}\left(\left(h_w\left(x^{(i)}\right) - y^{(i)}\right)x_i\right)$$

$$\}$$

It is important that these update rules are applied simultaneously, that is, they are both applied in the same iteration, so the new values of both w_0 and w_1 are plugged back in the next iteration. This is sometimes called **batch gradient descent** because it updates all the training samples in one *batch*.

It is fairly straightforward to apply these update rules on linear regression problems that have multiple features. This is true if we do not worry about the precise derivations.

For multiple features, our hypothesis function will look like this:

$$h_w\left(x\right) = w^T x = w_0 x_0 + w_1 x_1 + w_2 x_2 + \cdots + w_n x_n$$

Here, $x_0 = 1$, often called our **bias feature**, is added to help us with the following calculations. We see can see that, by using vectors, we can also write this as simply the transpose of the parameter values multiplied by the feature value vector, x. With multiple feature gradient descents, our cost function will apply to a vector of the parameter values, rather than just a single parameter. This is the new cost function.

$$J\left(w\right) = \frac{1}{2m}\sum_{i=1}^{m}\left(h_w\left(x^{(i)}\right) - y^{(i)}\right)^2$$

$J(w)$ is simply $J(w_0, w_1 ..., w_n)$, where n is the number of features. J is a function of the parameter vector, w. Now, our gradient descent update rule is as follows:

$$update\ w_j\ for\ j = (0, ..., n) \left\{ w_j : -w_j - \alpha \frac{1}{m} \alpha \sum_{i=1}^{m} \left(x^{(i)} - y^{(i)} \right) x_j^{(i)} \right\}$$

Notice that we now have multiple features. Therefore, we write the x value with the subscript j to indicate the jth feature. We can break this apart and see that it really represents the $j + 1$ nested update rules. Each one is identical, apart from their subscripts, to the training rule that we used for single features.

An important point to mention here, and one that we will revisit in later chapters, is that, to make our models work more efficiently, we can define our own features. For a simple situation, where our hypothesis is to estimate the price of a block of land based on two features, width and depth, obviously, we can multiply these two features to get one feature, that is, area. So, depending on a particular insight that you might have about a problem, it can make more sense to use derived features. We can take this idea further and create our own features to enable our model to fit nonlinear data. A technique to do this is **polynomial regression**. This involves adding power terms to our hypothesis function, making it a polynomial. Here is an example:

$$h_w(x) = w_0 + w_1 x + w_2 x^2 + w_3 x^3$$

A way to apply this, in the case of our land price example, is to simply add the square and the cube of our *area* feature. There are many possible choices for these terms, and in fact, a better choice in our housing example might be in taking the square root of one of the terms to stop the function exploding to infinity. This highlights an important point, that is, when using polynomial regression, we must be very careful about feature scaling. We can see that the terms in the function get increasingly larger as x gets larger.

We now have a model to fit nonlinear data, however, at this stage, we are just manually trying different polynomials. Ideally, we need to be able to incorporate feature selection, to some extent, in our models, rather than have a human try to figure out an appropriate function. We also need to be aware that correlated features may make our models unstable, so we need to devise ways of decomposing correlated features into their components. We look at these aspects in *Chapter 7, Features – How Algorithms See the World*.

The following is a simple implementation of batch gradient descent. Try running it with different values of the learning rate alpha, and on data with a greater bias and/or variance, and also after changing the number of iterations to see what effect this has on the performance of our model:

```python
import numpy as np
import random
import matplotlib.pyplot as plt


def gradientDescent(x, y, alpha, numIterations):
    xTrans = x.transpose()
    m, n = np.shape(x)
    theta = np.ones(n)
    for i in range(0, numIterations):
        hwx = np.dot(x, theta)
        loss = hwx - y
        cost = np.sum(loss ** 2) / (2 * m)
        print("Iteration %d | Cost: %f " % (i, cost))
        gradient = np.dot(xTrans, loss) / m
        theta = theta - alpha * gradient
    return theta


def genData(numPoints, bias, variance):
    x = np.zeros(shape=(numPoints, 2))
    y = np.zeros(shape=numPoints)
    for i in range(0, numPoints):
        x[i][0] = 1
        x[i][1] = i
        y[i] = (i + bias) + random.uniform(0, 1) * variance
    return x, y


def plotData(x,y,theta):
    plt.scatter(x[...,1],y)
    plt.plot(x[...,1],[theta[0] + theta[1]*xi for xi in x[...,1]])


x, y = genData(20, 25, 10)
```

```
iterations= 10000
alpha = 0.001
theta=gradientDescent(x,y,alpha,iterations)
plotData(x,y,theta)
```

The output of the code is as shown in the following screenshot:

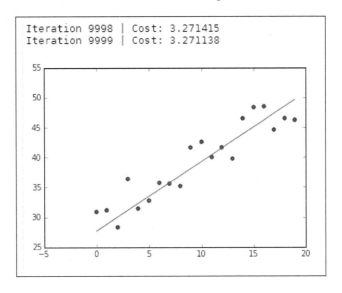

This is called **batch gradient descent** because, on each iteration, it updates the parameter values based on all the training samples at once. With **Stochastic gradient descent**, on the other hand, the gradient is approximated by the gradient of a single example at a time. Several passes may be made over the data until the algorithm converges. On each pass, the data is shuffled to prevent it from getting stuck in a loop. Stochastic gradient descent has been successfully applied to large scale learning problems such as natural language processing. One of the disadvantages is that it requires a number of hyper parameters, although this does present opportunities for tweaking such as choosing a loss function or the type of regularization applied. Stochastic gradient descent is also sensitive to feature scaling. Many implementations of this, such as **SGDClassifier** and **SGDRegressor** from the `sklearn` package, will use an adaptive learning rate by default. This reduces the learning rate as the algorithm moves closer to the minimum. To make these algorithms work well, it is usually necessary to scale the data so that each value in the input vector, X, is scaled between 0 and 1 or between -1 and 1. Alternatively, ensure that the data values have a mean of 0 and a variance of 1. This is most easily done using the `StandardScaler` class from `sklearn.preprocessing`.

Gradient descent is not the only algorithm, and in many ways, it is not the most efficient way to minimize the cost function. There are a number of advanced libraries that will compute values for the parameters much more efficiently than if we implemented the gradient descent update rules manually. Fortunately, we do not have to worry too much about the details because there are a number of sophisticated and efficient algorithms for regression already written in Python. For example, in the `sklearn.linear_model` module, there are the **Ridge**, **Lasso**, and **ElasticNet** algorithms that may perform better, depending on your application.

The normal equation

Let's now look at the linear regression problem from a slightly different angle. As I mentioned earlier, there is a numerical solution; thus, rather than iterate through our training set, as we do with gradient descent, we can use what is called the **normal equation** to solve it in one step. If you know some calculus, you will recall that we can minimize a function by taking its derivative and then setting the derivative to zero to solve for a variable. This makes sense because, if we consider our convex cost function, the minimum will be where the slope of the tangent is zero. So, in our simple case with one feature, we differentiate $J(w)$ with respect to w and set it to zero and solve for w. The problem we are interested in is when w is an $n+1$ parameter vector and the cost function, $J(w)$, is a function of this vector. One way to minimize this is to take the partial derivative of $J(w)$ for the parameter values in turn and then set these derivatives to zero, solving for each value of w. This gives us the values of w that are needed to minimize the cost function.

It turns out that an easy way to solve, what could be a long and complicated calculation, is what is known as the normal equation. To see how this works, we first define a feature matrix, shown as follows:

$$X = \begin{matrix} x_0^{(1)} & x_1^{(1)} & x_2^{(1)} & \cdots & x_n^{(1)} \\ x_0^{(2)} & x_1^{(2)} & x_2^{(2)} & \cdots & x_n^{(2)} \\ \cdots & \cdots & \cdots & \cdots & \cdots \\ x_0^{(m)} & x_1^{(m)} & x_2^{(m)} & \cdots & x_n^{(m)} \end{matrix}$$

This creates an *m* by *n + 1* matrix, where *m* is the number of training examples, and *n* is the number of features. Notice that, in our notation, we now define our training label vector as follows:

$$y = \begin{matrix} y^{(1)} \\ y^{(2)} \\ \cdots \\ y^{(m)} \end{matrix}$$

Now, it turns out that we can compute the parameter values to minimize this cost function by the following equation:

$$w = \left(X^T X \right)^{-1} X^T y$$

This is the normal equation. There are of course many ways to implement this in Python. Here is one simple way using the NumPy `matrix` class. Most implementations will have a regularization parameter that, among other things, prevents an error arising from attempting to transpose a singular matrix. This will occur when we have more features than training data, that is, when *n* is greater than *m*; the normal equation without regularization will not work. This is because the matrix $X^T X$ is non-transposable, and so, there is no way to calculate our term, $(X^T X)^{-1}$. Regularization has other benefits, as we will see shortly:

```python
import numpy as np

def normDemo(la=.9):
    X = np.matrix('1 2 5 ; 1 4 6')
    y=np.matrix('8; 16')
    xtrans=X.T
    idx=np.matrix(np.identity(X.shape[1]))
    xti = (xtrans.dot(X)+la * idx).I
    xtidt = xti.dot(xtrans)
    return(xtidt.dot(y))
```

One of the advantages of using the normal equation is that you do not need to worry about feature scaling. Features that have different ranges (for example, if one feature has values between 1 and 10, and another feature has values between zero and 1000) will likely cause problems for gradient descent. Using the normal equation, you do not need to worry about this. Another advantage of the normal equation is that you do not need to choose the learning rate. We saw that, with gradient descent; an incorrectly chosen learning rate could either make the model unnecessarily slow or, if the learning rate is too large, it can cause the model to overshoot the minimum. This may entail an extra step in our testing phase for gradient descent.

The normal equation has its own particular disadvantages; foremost is that it does not scale as well when we have data with a large number of features. We need to calculate the inverse of the transpose of our feature matrix, X. This calculation results in an n by n matrix. Remember that n is the number of features. This actually means that on most platforms the time it takes to invert a matrix grows, approximately, as a cube of n. So, for data with a large number of features, say greater than 10,000, you should probably consider using gradient descent rather than the normal equation. Another problem that arises when using the normal equation is that, when we have more features than training data, that is, when n is greater than m, the normal equation without regularization will not work. This is because the matrix, X^TX, is non-transposable, and so there is no way to calculate our term, $(X^TX)-1$.

Logistic regression

With our least squares model, we have applied it to solve the minimization problem. We can also use a variation of this idea to solve classification problems. Consider what happens when we apply linear regression to a classification problem. Let's take the simple case of binary classification with one feature. We can plot our feature on the x axis against the class labels on the y axis. Our feature variable is continuous, but our target variable on the y axis is discrete. For binary classification, we usually represent a *0* for the negative class, and a *1* for the positive class. We construct a regression line through the data and use a threshold on the y axis to estimate the decision boundary. Here we use a threshold of 0.5.

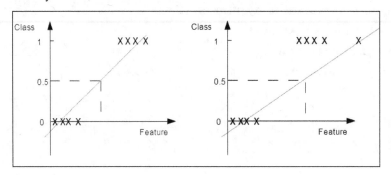

In the figure on the left-hand side, where the variance is small and our positive and negative cases are well separated, we get an acceptable result. The algorithm correctly classifies the training set. In the image on the right-hand side, we have a single outlier in the data. This makes our regression line flatter and shifts our cutoff to the right. The outlier, which clearly belongs in class *1*, should not make any difference to the model's prediction, however, now with the same cutoff point, the prediction misclassifies the first instance of class *1* as class *0*.

One way that we approach the problem is to formulate a different hypothesis representation. For logistic regression, we are going use the linear function as an input to another function, *g*.

$$h_w(x) = g\left(W^T x\right) where\ 0 \le h_w \le 1$$

The term *g* is called the **sigmoid** or **logistic function**. You will notice from its graph that, on the *y* axis, it has asymptotes at zero and one, and it crosses the axis at *0.5*.

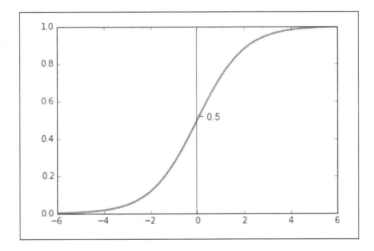

Now, if we replace the *z* with $W^T x$, we can rewrite our hypothesis function like this:

$$h_w(x) = \frac{1}{\left(1 + e^{-w^T x}\right)}$$

As with linear regression, we need to fit the parameters, w, to our training data to give us a function that can make predictions. Before we try and fit the model, let's look at how we can interpret the output from our hypothesis function. Since this will return a number between zero and one, the most natural way to interpret this is as it being the probability of the positive class. Since we know, or assume, that each sample can only belong in one of two classes, then the probability of the positive class plus the probability of the negative class must be equal to one. Therefore, if we can estimate the positive class, then we can estimate the probability of the negative class. Since we are ultimately trying to predict the class of a particular sample, we can interpret the output of the hypothesis function as positive if it returns a value greater than or equal to 0.5, or negative otherwise. Now, given the characteristics of the sigmoid function, we can write the following:

$$h_x = g\left(W^T x\right) \geq 0.5 \ whenever \ W^T x \geq 0$$

Whenever our hypothesis function, on a particular training sample, returns a number greater than or equal to zero, we can predict a positive class. Let's look at a simple example. We have not yet fitted our parameters to this model, and we will do so shortly, but for the sake of this example, let's assume that we have a parameter vector as follows:

$$W = \begin{matrix} -3 \\ 1 \\ 1 \end{matrix}$$

Our hypothesis function, therefore, looks like this:

$$h_w\left(x\right) = g\left(-3 + x_1 + x_2\right)$$

We can predict $y = 1$ if the following condition is met:

$$-3 + x_1 + x_2 \geq 0$$

Equivalently:

$$x_1 + x_2 \geq 3$$

This can be sketched with the following graph:

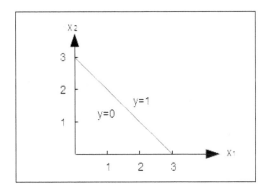

This is simply a straight line between x=3 and y=3, and it represents the **decision boundary**. It creates two regions where we predict either y = 0 or y = 1. What happens when the decision boundary is not a straight line? In the same way that we added polynomials to the hypothesis function in linear regression, we can also do this with logistic regression. Let's write a new hypothesis function with some higher order terms to see how we can fit it to the data:

$$h_w\left(x\right) = g\left(w_0 + w_1 x_1 + w_2 x_2 + w_3 x_1^2 + w_4 x_2^2\right)$$

Here we have added two squared terms to our function. We will see how to fit the parameters shortly, but for now, let's set our parameter vector to the following:

$$w = \begin{array}{c} -1 \\ 0 \\ 0 \\ 1 \\ 1 \end{array}$$

So, we can now write the following:

$$Predict\ y = 1\ if\ -1 + x_1^2 + x_2^2 \geq 0$$

Or alternatively, we can write this:

$$Predict \ y = 1 \ if \ x_1^2 + x_2^2 = 1$$

This, you may recognize, is the equation for a circle centered around the origin, and we can use this as our decision boundary. We can create more complex decision boundaries by adding higher order polynomial terms.

The Cost function for logistic regression

Now, we need to look at the important task of fitting the parameters to the data. If we rewrite the cost function we used for linear regression more simply, we can see that the cost is one half of the squared error:

$$Cost\left(h_w\left(x\right), y\right) = \frac{1}{2}\left(h_w\left(x\right) - y\right)^2$$

The interpretation is that it is simply calculating the cost we want the model to incur, given a certain prediction, that is, $h_w(x)$, and a training label, y.

This will work to a certain extent with logistic regression, however, there is a problem. With logistic regression, our hypothesis function is dependent on the nonlinear sigmoid function, and when we plot this against our parameters, it will usually produce a function that is not convex. This means that, when we try to apply an algorithm such as gradient descent to the cost function, it will not necessarily converge to the global minimum. A solution is to define a cost function that is convex, and it turns out that the following two functions, one for each class, are suitable for our purposes:

$$Cost\left(h_w\left(x\right)\right) = -\log\left(h_x\left(w\right)\right) if \ y = 1 \ Cost\left(h_w\left(x\right)\right) = -\log\left(1 - h_x\left(w\right)\right) if \ y = 0$$

This gives us the following graphs:

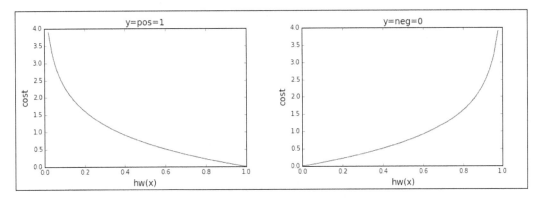

Intuitively, we can see that this does what we need it to do. If we consider a single training sample in the positive class, that is $y = 1$, and if our hypothesis function, $h_w(x)$, correctly predicts 1, then the cost, as you would expect, is 0. If the output of the hypothesis function is 0, it is incorrect, so the cost approaches infinity. When y is in the negative class, our cost function is the graph on the right. Here the cost is zero when $h_w(x)$ is 0 and rises to infinity when $h_w(x)$ is 1. We can write this in a more compact way, remembering that y is either 0 or 1:

$$Cost\left(h_w\left(x\right),y\right)=-y\log\left(h_w\left(x\right)\right)-\left(1-y\right)\log\left(1-h_w\left(x\right)\right)$$

We can see that, for each of the possibilities, $y=1$ or $y=0$, the irrelevant term is multiplied by 0, leaving the correct term for each particular case. So, now we can write our cost function as follows:

$$J\left(w\right)=\frac{-1}{m}\left[\sum_{i=1}^{m}y^{(i)}\log h_w\left(x^{(i)}\right)+\left(1-y^{(i)}\right)\log\left(1-h_w\left(x^{(i)}\right)\right)\right]$$

So, if we are given a new, unlabeled value of x, how do we make a prediction? As with linear regression, our aim is to minimize the cost function, $J(w)$. We can use the same update rule that we used for linear regression, that is, using the partial derivative to find the slope, and when we rewrite the derivative, we get the following:

$$Repeat\ until\ convergance: W_j := W_j - \alpha \sum_{i=1}^{m}\left(h_w\left(x^{(i)}\right)-y^{(i)}\right)x_j^{(i)}$$

Multiclass classification

So far, we have just looked at binary classification. For multiclass classification, we assume that each instance belongs to only one class. A slightly different classification problem is where each sample can belong to more than one target class. This is called multi-label classification. We can employ similar strategies on each of these types of problem.

There are two basic approaches:

- One versus all
- One versus many

In the one versus all approach, a single multiclass problem is transformed into a number of binary classification problems. This is called the **one versus all** technique because we take each class in turn and fit a hypothesis function for that particular class, assigning a negative class to the other classes. We end up with different classifiers, each of which is trained to recognize one of the classes. We make a prediction given a new input by running all the classifiers and picking the classifier that predicts a class with the highest probability. To formalize it, we write the following:

$$h_w^{(i)}(x) \text{ for each class } i \text{ predict probability } y = i$$

To make a prediction, we pick the class that maximizes the following:

$$h_w^{(i)}(x)$$

With another approach called the **one versus one** method, a classifier is constructed for each pair of classes. When the model makes a prediction, the class that receives the most votes wins. This method is generally slower than the one versus many method, especially when there are a large number of classes.

All Sklearn classifiers implement multiclass classification. We saw this in *Chapter 2, Tools and Techniques*, with the K-nearest neighbors example, where we attempted to predict one of three classes using the iris dataset. Sklearn implements the one versus all algorithm using the `OneVsRestClassifier` class and the one versus one algorithm with `OneVsOneClassifier`. These are called **meta-estimators** because they take another estimator as an input. They have the advantage of being able to permit changing the way more than two classes are handled, and this can result in better performance, either in terms of computational efficiency, or generalization error.

In the following example, we use the SVC:

```
from sklearn import datasets
from sklearn.multiclass import OneVsRestClassifier, OneVsOneClassifier
from sklearn.svm import LinearSVC

X,y = datasets.make_classification(n_samples=10000, n_features=5)
X1,y1 = datasets.make_classification(n_samples=10000, n_features=5)
clsAll=OneVsRestClassifier(LinearSVC(random_state=0)).fit(X, y)
clsOne=OneVsOneClassifier(LinearSVC(random_state=0)).fit(X1, y1)
print("One vs all cost= %f" % clsAll.score(X,y))
print("One vs one cost= %f" % clsOne.score(X1,y1))
```

We will observe the following output:

```
One vs all cost= 0.947400
One vs one cost= 0.949200
```

Regularization

We mentioned earlier that linear regression can become unstable, that is, highly sensitive to small changes in the training data, if features are correlated. Consider the extreme case where two features are perfectly negatively correlated such that any increase in one feature is accompanied by an equivalent decrease in another feature. When we apply our linear regression algorithm to just these two features, it will result in a function that is constant, so this is not really telling us anything about the data. Alternatively, if the features are positively correlated, small changes in them will be amplified. Regularization helps moderate this.

We saw previously that we could get our hypothesis to more closely fit the training data by adding polynomial terms. As we add these terms, the shape of the function becomes more complicated, and this usually results in the hypothesis overfitting the training data and performing poorly on the test data. As we add features, either directly from the data or the ones we derive ourselves, it becomes more likely that the model will overfit the data. One approach is to discard features that we think are less important. However, we cannot know for certain, in advance, what features may contain relevant information. A better approach is to not discard features but rather to shrink them. Since we do not know how much information each feature contains, regularization reduces the magnitude of all the parameters.

We can simply add the term to the cost function.

$$ J_w = \frac{1}{2m} \sum_{i=1}^{m} \left(h_w\left(x^{(i)}\right) - y^{(i)} \right)^2 + \lambda \sum_{j=1}^{n} w_j^2 $$

The hyper parameter, **lambda,** controls a tradeoff between two goals — the need to fit the training data, and the need to keep the parameters small to avoid overfitting. We do not apply the regularization parameter to our bias feature, so we separate the update rule for the first feature and add a regularization parameter to all subsequent features. We can write it like this:

$$ \textit{Repeat until convergance} \left\{ w_j := w_j - \alpha \frac{1}{m} \sum_{i=1}^{m} \left(h_w\left(x^{(i)}\right) - y^{(i)} \right) x_0^{(i)} \right. $$

$$ \left. w_j := w_j - \alpha \frac{1}{m} \sum_{i=1}^{m} \left(h_w\left(x^{(i)}\right) - y^{(i)} \right) x_j^{(i)} + \frac{\lambda}{m} w_j \right\} $$

Here, we have added our regularization term, $\lambda\, w_j / m$. To see more clearly how this works, we can group all the terms that depend on wj, and our update rule can be rewritten as follows:

$$ w_j := w_j \left(1 - \alpha \frac{\lambda}{m} \right) - \alpha \frac{1}{m} \sum_{i=1}^{m} \left(h_w\left(x^{(i)}\right) - y^{(i)} \right) x_j^{(i)} $$

The regularization parameter, λ, is usually a small number greater than zero. In order for it to have the desired effect, it is set such that $a\,\lambda / m$ is a number slightly less than *1*. This will shrink w_j on each iteration of the update.

Now, let's see how we can apply regularization to the normal equation. The equation is as follows:

$$ w = \left(X^T X + \lambda I \right)^{-1} X^T y $$

This is sometimes referred to as the **closed form** solution. We add the identity matrix, *I*, multiplied by the regularization parameter. The identity matrix is an *(n+1)* by *(n+1)* matrix consisting of ones on the main diagonal and zeros everywhere else.

In some implementations, we might also make the first entry, the top-left corner, of the matrix zero reflect the fact that we are not applying a regularization parameter to the first bias feature. However, in practice, this will rarely make much difference to our model.

When we multiply it with the identity matrix, we get a matrix where the main diagonal contains the value of λ, with all other positions as zero. This makes sure that, even if we have more features than training samples, we will still be able to invert the matrix X^TX. It also makes our model more stable if we have correlated variables. This form of regression is sometimes called **ridge regression**, and we saw an implementation of this in *Chapter 2, Tools and Techniques*. An interesting alternative to ridge regression is **lasso regression**. It replaces the ridge regression regularization term, $\sum_i wi\,2$, with $\sum_i |\,wi\,|$. That is, instead of using the sum of the squares of the weights, it uses the sum of the average of the weights. The result is that some of the weights are set to 0 and others are shrunk. Lasso regressions tends to be quite sensitive to the regularization parameter. Unlike ridge regression, lasso regression does not have a closed-form solution, so other forms of numerical optimization need to be employed. Ridge regression is sometimes referred to as using the **L2 norm,** and lasso regularization, the **L1 norm**.

Finally, we will look at how to apply regularization to logistic regression. As with linear regression, logistic regression can suffer from the same problems of overfitting if our hypothesis functions contain higher-order terms or many features. We can modify our logistic regression cost function to add the regularization parameter, as shown as follows:

$$J_w = -\left[\frac{1}{m}\sum_{i=1}^{m} y^{(i)}logh_w\left(x^{(i)}\right) + \left(1 - y^{(i)}\right)log\left(1 - h_w\left(x^{(i)}\right)\right)\right] + \frac{\lambda}{2}m\sum_{j=1}^{n} w_j^2$$

To implement gradient descent for logistic regression, we end up with an equation that, on the surface, looks identical to the one we used for gradient descent for linear regression. However, we must remember that our hypothesis function is the one we used for logistic regression.

$$w_j := w_j - \alpha\frac{1}{m}\sum_{i=1}^{m}\left(h_w\left(x^{(i)}\right) - y^{(i)}\right)x_j^{(i)} + \frac{\lambda}{m}w_j$$

Using the hypothesis function, we get the following:

$$h_w(x) = \frac{1}{\left(1 + e^{-W^T}x\right)}$$

Summary

In this chapter, we studied some of the most used techniques in machine learning. We created hypothesis representations for linear and logistic regression. You learned how to create a cost function to measure the performance of the hypothesis on training data, and how to minimize the cost function in order to fit the parameters, using both gradient descent and the normal equation. We showed how you could fit the hypothesis function to nonlinear data by using polynomial terms in the hypothesis function. Finally, we looked at regularization, its uses, and how to apply it to logistic and linear regression.

These are powerful techniques used widely in many different machine learning algorithms. However, as you have probably realized, there is a lot more to the story. The models we have looked at so far usually require considerable human intervention to get them to perform usefully. For example, we have to set the hyper parameters, such as the learning rate or regularization parameter, and, in the case of non linear data, we have to try and find polynomial terms that will force our hypothesis to fit the data. It will be difficult to determine exactly what these terms are, especially when we have many features. In the next chapter, we will look at the ideas that drive some of the most powerful learning algorithms on the planet, that is, neural networks.

6
Neural Networks

Artificial neural networks, as the name suggests, are based algorithms that attempt to mimic the way neurons work in the brain. Conceptual work began in the 1940s, but it is only somewhat recently that a number of important insights, together with the availability of hardware to run these more computationally expensive models, have given neural networks practical application. They are now state-of-the-art techniques that are at the heart of many advanced machine learning applications.

In this chapter, we will introduce the following topics:

- Logistic units
- The cost function for neural networks
- Implementing a neural network
- Other neural network architectures

Getting started with neural networks

We saw in the last chapter how we could create a nonlinear decision boundary by adding polynomial terms to our hypothesis function. We can also use this technique in linear regression to fit nonlinear data. However, this is not the ideal solution for a number of reasons. Firstly, we have to choose polynomial terms, and for complicated decision boundaries, this can be an imprecise and time-intensive process, which can take quite a bit of trial and error. We also need to consider what happens when we have a large number of features. It becomes difficult to understand exactly how added polynomial terms will change the decision boundary. It also means that the possible number of derived features will grow exponentially. To fit complicated boundaries, we will need many higher-order terms, and our model will become unwieldy, computationally expensive, and hard to understand.

Consider applications such as computer vision, where in a gray scale image, each pixel is a feature that has a value between 0 and 255. For a small image, say 100 pixels by 100 pixels, we have 10,000 features. If we include just quadratic terms, we end up with around 50 million possible features, and to fit complex decision boundaries, we likely need cubic and higher order terms. Clearly, such a model is entirely unworkable.

When we approach the problem of trying to mimic the brain, we are faced with a number of difficulties. Considering all the different things that the brain does, we might first think that the brain consists of a number of different algorithms, each specialized to do a particular task, and each hard wired into different parts of the brain. This approach basically considers the brain as a number of subsystems, each with its own program and task. For example, the auditory cortex for perceiving sound has its own algorithm that, for example, does a **Fourier** transform on the incoming sound wave to detect pitch. The visual cortex, on the other hand, has its own distinct algorithm for decoding and converting the signals from the optic nerve into the sense of sight. There is, however, growing evidence that the brain does not function like this at all.

Recent experiments on animals have shown the remarkable adaptabilities of brain tissue. Rewiring the optic nerve to the auditory cortex in animals, scientists found that the brain could learn to see using the machinery of the auditory cortex. The animals were tested to have full vision despite the fact that their visual cortex had been bypassed. It appears that brain tissue, in different parts of the brain, can relearn how to interpret its inputs. So, rather than the brain consisting of specialized subsystems programmed to perform specific tasks, it uses the same algorithm to learn different tasks. This single algorithm approach has many advantages, not least of which is that it is relatively easy to implement. It also means that we can create generalized models and then train them to perform specialized tasks. Like in real brains using a single algorithm to describe how each neuron communicates with the other neurons around it, it allows artificial neural networks to be adaptable and able to carry out multiple higher-level tasks. But, what is the nature of this single algorithm?

When trying to mimic real brain functions, we are forced to greatly simplify many things. For example, there is no way to take into account the role of the chemical state of the brain, or the state of the brain at different stages of development and growth. Most of the neural net models currently in use employ discrete layers of artificial neurons, or units, connected in a well ordered linear sequence or in layers. The brain, on the other hand, consists of many complex, nested, and interconnected neural circuits. Some progress has been made in attempting to imitate these complex feedback systems, and we will look at these at the end of this chapter. However, there is still much that we do not know about real brain action and how to incorporate this complex behavior into artificial neural networks.

Logistic units

As a starting point, we use the idea of a logistic unit over the simplified model of a neuron. It consists of a set of inputs and outputs and an activation function. This activation function is essentially performing a calculation on the set of inputs, and subsequently giving an output. Here, we set the activation function to the sigmoid that we used for logistic regression in the previous chapter:

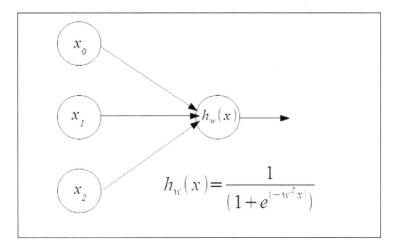

We have Two input units, x_1 and x_2 and a bias unit, x_0, that is set to one. These are fed into a hypothesis function that uses the sigmoid logistic function and a weight vector, w, which parameterizes the hypothesis function. The feature vector, consisting of binary values, and the parameter vector for the preceding example consist of the following:

$$
\begin{matrix}
x_0 = 1 & W_0 \\
x = x_1 & W = W_1 \\
x_2 & W_2 \\
x_3 & W_3
\end{matrix}
$$

To see how we can get this to perform logical functions, let's give the model some weights. We can write this as a function of the sigmoid, g, and our weights. To get started, we are just going to choose some weights. We will learn shortly how to train the model to learn its own weights. Let's say that we set out weight such that we have the following hypothesis function:

$$
h_w(x) = g\left(-15 + 10_{x_1} + 10_{x_2}\right)
$$

We feed our model some simple labeled data and construct a truth table:

$$
\begin{array}{ccccc}
x_1 & x_2 & y & & h_w(x) \\
0 & 0 & 1 & & g(-15) \approx 0 \\
0 & 1 & 0 & & g(-5) \approx 0 \\
1 & 0 & 0 & & g(-5) \approx 0 \\
1 & 1 & 1 & & g(5) \approx 1 \\
\end{array}
$$

Although this data appears relatively simple, the decision boundary that is needed to separate the classes is not. Our target variable, y, forms the logical **XNOR** with the input variables. The output is *1* only when both x_1 and x_2 are either *0* or *1*.

Here, our hypothesis has given us a logical **AND**. That is, it returns a *1* when both x_1 and x_2 are *1*. By setting the weights to other values, we can get our single artificial neuron to form other logical functions.

This gives us the logical **OR** function:

$$
h_w = -5 + 10x_1 + 10x_2
$$

To perform an XNOR, we combine the AND, OR, and NOT functions. To perform negation, that is, a logical **NOT**, we simply choose large negative weights for the input variable that we want to negate.

Logistics units are connected together to form artificial neural networks. These networks consist of an input layer, one or more hidden layers, and an output layer. Each unit has an activation function, here the sigmoid, and is parameterized by the weight matrix W:

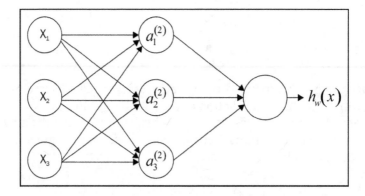

We can write out the activation functions for each of the units in the hidden layer:

$$a_1^{(2)} = g\left(W_{10}^{(1)}x_0 + W_{11}^{(1)}x_1 + W_{12}^{(1)}x_2 + W_{13}^{(1)}x_3\right)$$

$$a_2^{(2)} = g\left(W_{20}^{(1)}x_0 + W_{21}^{(1)}x_1 + W_{22}^{(1)}x_2 + W_{23}^{(1)}x_3\right)$$

$$a_3^{(2)} = g\left(W_{30}^{(1)}x_0 + W_{31}^{(1)}x_1 + W_{32}^{(1)}x_2 + W_{33}^{(1)}x_3\right)$$

The activation function for the output layer is as follows:

$$h_w(x) = a_1^{(3)} = g\left(W_{10}^{(2)}a_0^{(2)} + W_{11}^{(2)}a_1^{(2)} + W_{12}^{(2)}a_2^{(2)} + W_{13}^{(2)}a_3^{(2)}\right)$$

More generally, we can say a function mapping from a given layer, j, to the layer $j+1$ is determined by the parameter matrix, W^j. The super script j represents the jth layer, and the subscript, i, denotes the unit in that layer. We denote the parameter or weight matrix, $W^{(j)}$, which governs the mapping from the layer j to the layer $j + 1$. We denote the individual weights in the subscript of their matrix index.

Note that the dimensions of the parameter matrix for each layer will be the number of units in the next layer multiplied by the number of units in the current layer plus 1; this is for x_0, which is the bias layer. More formally, we can write the dimension of the parameter matrix for a given layer, j, as follows:

$$d_{(j+1)} \times d_j + 1$$

The subscript $(j + 1)$ refers to the number of units in the next input layer and the forward layer, and the $d_j + 1$ refers to the number of units in the current layer plus 1.

Let's now look at how we can calculate these activation functions using a vector implementation. We can write these functions more compactly by defining a new term, Z, which consists of the weighted linear combination of the input values for each unit on a given layer. Here is an example:

$$a_{(1)}^2 = g\left(Z_1^{(2)}\right)$$

We are just replacing everything in the inner term of our activation function with a single function, Z. Here, the super script *(2)* represents the layer number, and the subscript *1* indicates the unit in that layer. So, more generally, the matrix that defines the activation function for the layer *j* is as follows:

$$= Z_1^{(j)}$$
$$Z^{(j)} = Z_2^{(j)}$$
$$..$$
$$= Z_n^{(j)}$$

So, in our three layer example, our output layer can be defined as follows:

$$h_w(x) = a^{(3)} = g(z(3))$$

We can learn features by first looking at just the three units on the single hidden layer and how it maps its input to the input of the single unit on the output layer. We can see that it is only performing logistic regression using the set of features (a^2). The difference is that now the input features of the hidden layer have themselves been computed using the weights learned from the raw features at the input layer. Through hidden layers, we can start to fit more complicated nonlinear functions.

We can solve our XNOR problem using the following neural net architecture:

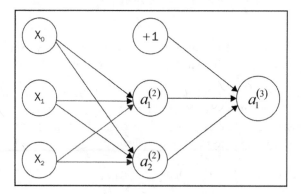

Here, we have three units on the input layer, two units plus the bias unit on the single hidden layer, and one unit on the output layer. We can set the weights for the first unit in the hidden layer (not including the bias unit) to perform the logical function x_1 AND x_2. The weights for the second unit perform the functions (NOT x_1) AND (NOT x_2). Finally, our output layer performs the OR function.

We can write our activation functions as follows:

$$a_1^{(2)} = g\left(-15x_0 + 10x_1 + 10x_2\right)$$
$$a_2^{(2)} = g\left(10x_0 + 20x_1 - 20x_2\right)$$
$$a_1^{(3)} = g\left(-5x_0 + 10x_1 + 10x_2\right)$$

The truth table for this network looks like this:

x_1	x_2	$a_1^{(2)}$	$a_2^{(2)}$	$h_w(x)$
0	0	0	1	1
0	1	0	0	0
1	0	0	0	0
1	1	1	0	1

To perform multiclass classification with neural networks, we use architectures with an output unit for each class that we are trying to classify. The network outputs a vector of binary numbers with 1 indicating that the class is present. This output variable is an i dimensional vector, where i is the number of output classes. The output space for four features, for example, would look like this:

$y^{(1)}$		$y^{(2)}$		$y^{(3)}$		$y^{(4)}$
1		0		0		0
0	;	1	;	0	;	0
0		0		1		0
0		0		0		1

Our goal is to define a hypothesis function to approximately equal one of these four vectors:

$$h_w(x) \approx y^{(i)}$$

This is essentially a one versus all representation.

We can describe a neural network architecture by the number of layers, L, and by the number of units in each layer by a number, s_i, where the subscript indicates the layer number. For convenience, I am going to define a variable, t, indicating the number of units on the layer $l + 1$, where $l + 1$ is the forward layer, that is, the layer to the right-hand side of the diagram.

Cost function

To fit the weights in a neural net for a given training set, we first need to define a cost function:

$$J_w = \frac{-1}{m}[\sum_{i=1}^{m}\sum_{k=1}^{k} y_k^{(i)} log\left(h_w\left(x^{(i)}\right)\right)_k + \left(1-y_k^{(i)}\right) log\left(1-\left(h_w\left(x^{(i)}\right)\right)_k\right) + \frac{\lambda}{2}m\sum_{l=1}^{L-1}\sum_{i=1}^{s}\sum_{j=1}^{t}\left(W_{ji}^{(l)}\right)^2$$

This is very similar to the cost function we used for logistic regression, except that now we are also summing over k output units. The triple summation used in the regularization term looks a bit complicated, but all it is really doing is summing over each of the terms in the parameter matrix, and using this to calculate the regularization. Note that the summation, i, l, and j start at 1, rather than 0; this is to reflect the fact that we do not apply regularization to the bias unit.

Minimizing the cost function

Now that we have cost function, we need to work out a way to minimize it. As with gradient descent, we need to compute the partial derivatives to calculate the slope of the cost function. This is done using the **back propagation** algorithm. It is called back propagation because we begin by calculating the error at the output layer, then calculating the error for each previous layer in turn. We can use these derivatives calculated by the cost function to work out parameter values for each of the units in our neural network. To do this, we need to define an error term:

$$\delta_j^{(l)} = error\ of\ node\ j\ in\ layer\ |$$

For this example, let's assume that we have a total of three layers, including the input and output layers. The error at the output layer can be written as follows:

$$\delta_j^{(3)} = a_j^{(3)} - y_j = h_w(x) - y_j$$

The activation function in the final layer is equivalent to our hypothesis function, and we can use simple vector subtraction to calculate the difference between the values predicted by our hypothesis, and the actual values in our training set. Once we know the error in our output layer, we are able to *back propagate* to find the error, which is the delta values, in previous layers:

$$\delta^{(2)} = \left(W^{(2)}\right)^T \delta^{(3)} . * g'\left(z^{(2)}\right)$$

This will calculate the error for layer three. We use the transpose of the parameter vector of the current layer, in this example layer 2, multiplied by the error vector from the forward layer, in this case layer 3. We then use pairwise multiplication, indicated by the * symbol, with the derivative of the activation function, *g*, evaluated at the input values given by $z^{(3)}$. We can calculate this derivative term by the following:

$$g'\left(z^{(3)}\right) = a^{(3)} . * \left(1 - a^{(3)}\right)$$

If you know calculus, it is a fairly straight forward procedure to prove this, but for our purposes, we will not go into it here. As you would expect when we have more than one hidden layer, we can calculate the delta values for each hidden layer in exactly the same way, using the parameter vector, the delta vector for the forward layer, and the derivative of the activation function for the current layer. We do not need to calculate the delta values for layer 1 because these are just the features themselves without any errors. Finally, through a rather complicated mathematical proof that we will not go into here, we can write the derivative of the cost function, ignoring regularization, as follows:

$$\frac{\partial}{\left[\partial W_{ij}^{(l)}\right]} J(W) = a_j^{(l)} \delta_i^{(l+1)}$$

By computing the delta terms using back propagation, we can find these partial derivatives for each of the parameter values. Now, let's see how we apply this to a dataset of training samples. We need to define capital delta, Δ, which is just the matrix of the delta terms and has the dimensions, $l{:}i{:}j$. This will act as an **accumulator** of the delta values from each node in the neural network, as the algorithm loops through each training sample. Within each loop, it performs the following functions on each training sample:

1. It sets the activation functions in the first layer to each value of x, that is, our input features.

2. It performs forward propagation on each subsequent layer in turn up to the output layer to calculate the activation functions for each layer.

3. It computes the delta values at the output layer and begins the process of back propagation. This is similar to the process we performed in forward propagation, except that it occurs in reverse. So, for our output layer in our 3-layer example, it is demonstrated as follows:

$$\delta^{(3)} = a^{(3)} - y^{(i)}$$

Remember that this is all happening in a loop, so we are dealing with one training sample at a time; $y^{(i)}$ represents the target value of the ith training sample. We can now use the back propagation algorithm to calculate the delta values for previous layers. We can now add these values to the accumulator, using the update rule:

$$\Delta^{(l)}_{(ij)} := \Delta^{(l)}_{(ij)} + a^{(l)}_j \delta^{(l+1)}$$

This formula can be expressed in its vectorized form, updating all training samples at once, as shown:

$$\Delta^{(l)} := \Delta^{(l)} + \delta^{(l+1)} \left(a^{(l)} \right)^T$$

Now, we can add our regularization term:

$$\Delta^{(i)} := +\Delta^{(i)} + \lambda^{(i)}$$

Finally, we can update the weights by performing gradient descent:

$$W^{(l)} := W^{(l)} - \alpha \Delta^{(l)}$$

Remember that *a* is the learning rate, that is, a hyper parameter we set to a small number between 0 and 1.

Implementing a neural network

There is one more thing we need to consider, and that is the initialization of our weights. If we initialize them to 0, or all to the same number, all the units on the forward layer will be computing the same function at the input, making the calculation highly redundant and unable to fit complex data. In essence, what we need to do is break the symmetry so that we give each unit a slightly different starting point that actually allows the network to create more interesting functions.

Now, let's look at how we might implement this in code. This implementation is written by Sebastian Raschka, taken from his excellent book, *Python Machine Learning*, released by Packt Publishing:

```python
import numpy as np
from scipy.special import expit
import sys


class NeuralNetMLP(object):

    def __init__(self, n_output, n_features, n_hidden=30,
                 l1=0.0, l2=0.0, epochs=500, eta=0.001,
                 alpha=0.0, decrease_const=0.0, shuffle=True,
                 minibatches=1, random_state=None):

        np.random.seed(random_state)
        self.n_output = n_output
        self.n_features = n_features
        self.n_hidden = n_hidden
        self.w1, self.w2 = self._initialize_weights()
        self.l1 = l1
        self.l2 = l2
        self.epochs = epochs
        self.eta = eta
        self.alpha = alpha
```

```
        self.decrease_const = decrease_const
        self.shuffle = shuffle
        self.minibatches = minibatches


    def _encode_labels(self, y, k):

        onehot = np.zeros((k, y.shape[0]))
        for idx, val in enumerate(y):
            onehot[val, idx] = 1.0
        return onehot


    def _initialize_weights(self):
        """Initialize weights with small random numbers."""
        w1 = np.random.uniform(-1.0, 1.0, size=self.n_hidden*(self.n_
features + 1))
        w1 = w1.reshape(self.n_hidden, self.n_features + 1)
        w2 = np.random.uniform(-1.0, 1.0, size=self.n_output*(self.n_
hidden + 1))
        w2 = w2.reshape(self.n_output, self.n_hidden + 1)
        return w1, w2


    def _sigmoid(self, z):

        # return 1.0 / (1.0 + np.exp(-z))
        return expit(z)


    def _sigmoid_gradient(self, z):
        sg = self._sigmoid(z)
        return sg * (1 - sg)


    def _add_bias_unit(self, X, how='column'):

        if how == 'column':
            X_new = np.ones((X.shape[0], X.shape[1]+1))
            X_new[:, 1:] = X
```

```python
    elif how == 'row':
        X_new = np.ones((X.shape[0]+1, X.shape[1]))
        X_new[1:, :] = X
    else:
        raise AttributeError('`how` must be `column` or `row`')
    return X_new


def _feedforward(self, X, w1, w2):

    a1 = self._add_bias_unit(X, how='column')
    z2 = w1.dot(a1.T)
    a2 = self._sigmoid(z2)
    a2 = self._add_bias_unit(a2, how='row')
    z3 = w2.dot(a2)
    a3 = self._sigmoid(z3)
    return a1, z2, a2, z3, a3


def _L2_reg(self, lambda_, w1, w2):
    """Compute L2-regularization cost"""
    return (lambda_/2.0) * (np.sum(w1[:, 1:] ** 2) + np.sum(w2[:, 1:]
** 2))


def _L1_reg(self, lambda_, w1, w2):
    """Compute L1-regularization cost"""
    return (lambda_/2.0) * (np.abs(w1[:, 1:]).sum() + np.abs(w2[:,
1:]).sum())


def _get_cost(self, y_enc, output, w1, w2):

    term1 = -y_enc * (np.log(output))
    term2 = (1 - y_enc) * np.log(1 - output)
    cost = np.sum(term1 - term2)
    L1_term = self._L1_reg(self.l1, w1, w2)
    L2_term = self._L2_reg(self.l2, w1, w2)
    cost = cost + L1_term + L2_term
```

```
        return cost


    def _get_gradient(self, a1, a2, a3, z2, y_enc, w1, w2):

        # backpropagation
        sigma3 = a3 - y_enc
        z2 = self._add_bias_unit(z2, how='row')
        sigma2 = w2.T.dot(sigma3) * self._sigmoid_gradient(z2)
        sigma2 = sigma2[1:, :]
        grad1 = sigma2.dot(a1)
        grad2 = sigma3.dot(a2.T)

        # regularize
        grad1[:, 1:] += (w1[:, 1:] * (self.l1 + self.l2))
        grad2[:, 1:] += (w2[:, 1:] * (self.l1 + self.l2))

        return grad1, grad2

    def predict(self, X):

        if len(X.shape) != 2:
            raise AttributeError('X must be a [n_samples, n_features]
array.\n'
                                 'Use X[:,None] for 1-feature
classification,'
                                 '\nor X[[i]] for 1-sample
classification')

        a1, z2, a2, z3, a3 = self._feedforward(X, self.w1, self.w2)
        y_pred = np.argmax(z3, axis=0)
        return y_pred

    def fit(self, X, y, print_progress=False):

        self.cost_ = []
        X_data, y_data = X.copy(), y.copy()
```

```
        y_enc = self._encode_labels(y, self.n_output)

        delta_w1_prev = np.zeros(self.w1.shape)
        delta_w2_prev = np.zeros(self.w2.shape)

        for i in range(self.epochs):

            # adaptive learning rate
            self.eta /= (1 + self.decrease_const*i)

            if print_progress:
                sys.stderr.write('\rEpoch: %d/%d' % (i+1, self.epochs))
                sys.stderr.flush()

            if self.shuffle:
                idx = np.random.permutation(y_data.shape[0])
                X_data, y_data = X_data[idx], y_data[idx]

            mini = np.array_split(range(y_data.shape[0]), self.
minibatches)
            for idx in mini:

                # feedforward
                a1, z2, a2, z3, a3 = self._feedforward(X[idx], self.w1,
self.w2)
                cost = self._get_cost(y_enc=y_enc[:, idx],
                                output=a3,
                                w1=self.w1,
                                w2=self.w2)
                self.cost_.append(cost)

                # compute gradient via backpropagation
                grad1, grad2 = self._get_gradient(a1=a1, a2=a2,
                                            a3=a3, z2=z2,
                                            y_enc=y_enc[:, idx],
```

```
                                          w1=self.w1,
                                          w2=self.w2)


        delta_w1, delta_w2 = self.eta * grad1, self.eta * grad2
        self.w1 -= (delta_w1 + (self.alpha * delta_w1_prev))
        self.w2 -= (delta_w2 + (self.alpha * delta_w2_prev))
        delta_w1_prev, delta_w2_prev = delta_w1, delta_w2


    return self
```

Now, let's apply this neural net to the iris sample dataset. Remember that this dataset contains three classes, so we set the `n_output` parameter (the number of output layers) to 3. The shape of the first axis in the dataset refers to the number of features. We create 50 hidden layers and 100 epochs, with each epoch being a complete loop over all the training set. Here, we set the learning rate, `alpha`, to `.001`, and we display a plot of the cost against the number of epochs:

```
iris = datasets.load_iris()
X=iris.data
y=iris.target
nn= NeuralNetMLP(3, X.shape[1],n_hidden=50, epochs=100, alpha=.001)
nn.fit(X,y)
plt.plot(range(len(nn.cost_)),nn.cost_)
plt.show()
```

Here is the output:

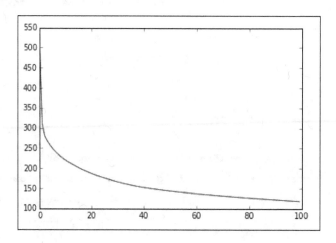

The graph shows how the cost is decreasing on each epoch. To get a feel for how the model works, spend some time experimenting with it on other data sets and with a variety of input parameters. One particular data set that is used often when testing multiclass classification problems is the MNIST dataset, which is available at `http://yann.lecun.com/exdb/mnist/`. This consists of datasets with 60,000 images of hand drawn letters, along with their labels. It is often used as a benchmark for machine learning algorithms.

Gradient checking

Back propagation, and neural nets in general, are a little difficult to conceptualize. So, it is often not easy to understand how changing any of the model (hyper) parameters will affect the outcome. Furthermore, with different implementations, it is possible to get results that indicate that an algorithm is working correctly, that is, the cost function is decreasing on each level of gradient descent. However, as with any complicated software, there can be hidden bugs that might only manifest themselves under very specific conditions. A way to help eliminate these is through a procedure called **gradient checking**. This is a numerical way of approximating gradients, and we can understand this intuitively by examining the following diagram:

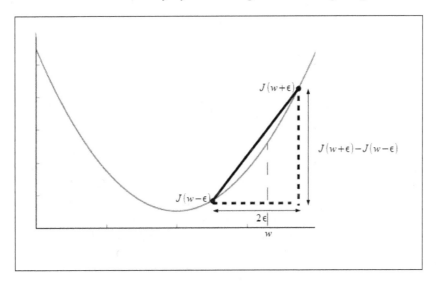

The derivative of *J(w)*, with respect to *w*, can be approximated as follows:

$$\frac{d}{dw}J(w) \approx \frac{\left(J(w+\epsilon) - J(w-\epsilon)\right)}{(2\epsilon)}$$

The preceding formula approximates the derivative when the parameter is a single value. We need to evaluate these derivatives on a cost function, where the weights are a vector. We do this by performing a partial derivative on each of the weights in turn. Here is an example:

$$w = \left[w_1, w_2, \ldots, w_n \right]$$

$$\frac{\partial}{\left(\partial w_n \right)} J\left(w \right) = J\left(w_1 + \epsilon, w_2, \ldots, w_n \right) - J\left(w_{-\epsilon}, w_2, \ldots, w_n \right)$$

$$\frac{\partial}{\left(\partial w_n \right)} J\left(w \right) = J\left(w_1, w_2, \ldots, w_n + \epsilon \right) - J\left(w, w_2, \ldots, w_n - \epsilon \right)$$

Other neural net architectures

Much of the most important work being done in the field of neural net models, and indeed machine learning in general, is using very complex neural nets with many layers and features. This approach is often called **deep architecture** or deep learning. Human and animal learning occurs at a rate and depth that no machine can match. Many of the elements of biological learning still remain a mystery. One of the key areas of research, and one of the most useful in practical applications, is that of object recognition. This is something quite fundamental to living systems, and higher animals have evolved an extraordinary ability to learn complex relationships between objects. Biological brains have many layers; each synaptic event exists in a long chain of synaptic processes. In order to recognize complex objects, such as people's faces or handwritten digits, a fundamental task that is needed is to create a hierarchy of representation from the raw input to higher and higher levels of abstraction. The goal is to transform raw data, such as a set of pixel values, into something we can describe as, say, *a person riding bicycle*. An approach to solving these sorts of problems is to use a sparse representation that creates higher dimensional feature spaces, where there are many features, but only very few of them have non-zero values. This approach is attractive for several reasons. Firstly, features may become more linearly separable in higher feature spaces. Also, it has been shown in certain models that sparsity can be used to make training more efficient and help extract information from very noisy data. We will explore this idea and the general concept of feature extraction in greater detail in the next chapter.

Another interesting idea is that of **recurrent neural networks** or **RNNs**. These are in many ways quite distinct from the feed forward networks that we have considered so far. Rather than simply static mappings between input and output, RNNs have at least one cyclic feedback path. RNNs introduce a time component to the network because a unit's input may include inputs that it received earlier via a feedback loop. All biological neural networks are highly recurrent. Artificial RNNs have shown promise in areas such as speech and hand writing recognition. However, they are, in general, much harder to train because we cannot simply back propagate the error. We have to take into consideration the time component and the dynamic, nonlinear characteristics of such systems. RNNs will provide a very interesting area for future research.

Summary

In this chapter, we introduced the powerful machine learning algorithms of artificial neural networks. We saw how these networks are a simplified model of neurons in the brain. They can perform complex learning tasks, such as learning highly nonlinear decision boundaries, using layers of artificial neurons, or units, to learn new features from labelled data. In the next chapter, we will look at the crucial component of any machine learning algorithm, that is, its features.

7
Features – How Algorithms See the World

So far in this book, we suggested a number of ways and a number of reasons for creating, extracting, or, otherwise, manipulating features. In this chapter, we will address this topic head on. The right features, sometimes called **attributes**, are the central component for machine learning models. A sophisticated model with the wrong features is worthless. Features are how our applications see the world. For all but the most simple tasks, we will process our features before feeding them to a model. There are many interesting ways in which we can do this, and it is such an important topic that it's appropriate to devote an entire chapter to it.

It has only been in the last decade or so that machine learning models have been routinely using tens of thousands of features or more. This allows us to tackle many different problems, such as those where our feature set is large compared to the number of samples. Two typical applications are genetic analysis and text categorization. For genetic analysis, our variables are a set of **gene expression coefficients**. These are based on the number of **mRNA** present in a sample, for example, taken from a tissue biopsy. A classification task might be performed to predict whether a patient has cancer or not. The number of training and test samples together may be a number less than 100. On the other hand, the number of variables in the raw data may range from 6,000 to 60,000. Not only will this translate to a large number of features, it also means that the range of values between features is quite large too. In this chapter, we will cover the following topics:

- Feature types
- Operations and statistics
- Structured features
- Transforming features
- Principle component analysis

Feature types

There are three distinct types of features: quantitative, ordinal, and categorical. We can also consider a fourth type of feature—the Boolean—as this type does have a few distinct qualities, although it is actually a type of categorical feature. These feature types can be ordered in terms of how much information they convey. Quantitative features have the highest information capacity followed by ordinal, categorical, and Boolean.

Let's take a look at the tabular analysis:

Feature type	Order	Scale	Tendency	Dispersion	Shape
Quantitative	Yes	Yes	Mean	Range, variance, and standard deviation	Skewness, kurtosis
Ordinal	Yes	No	Median	Quantiles	NA
Categorical	No	No	Mode	NA	NA

The preceding table shows the three types of features, their statistics, and properties. Each feature inherits the statistics from the features from the next row it in the table. For example, the measurement of central tendency for quantitative features includes the median and mode.

Quantitative features

The distinguishing characteristic of quantitative features is that they are continuous, and they usually involve mapping them to real numbers. Often, feature values can be mapped to a subset of real numbers, for example, expressing age in years; however, care must be taken to use the full scale when calculating statistics, such as mean or standard deviation. Because quantitative features have a meaningful numeric scale, they are often used in geometric models. When they are used in tree models, they result in a binary split, for example, using a threshold value where values above the threshold go to one child and values equal to or below the threshold go to the other child. Tree models are insensitive to monotonic transformations of scale, that is, transformations that do not change the ordering of the feature values. For example, it does not matter to a tree model if we measure length in centimeters or inches, or use a logarithmic or linear scale, we simply have to change the threshold values to the same scale. Tree models ignore the scale of quantitative features and treat them as ordinal. This is also true for rule-based models. For probabilistic models, such as the naïve Bayes classifier, quantitative features need to be discretized into a finite number of bins, and therefore, converted to categorical features.

Ordinal features

Ordinal features are features that have a distinct order but do not have a scale. They can be encoded as integer values; however, doing so does not imply any scale. A typical example is that of house numbers. Here, we can discern the position of a house on a street by its number. We assume that house number 1 will come before house number 20 and that houses with the numbers 10 and 11 would be located close to each other. However, the size of the number does not imply any scale; for example, there is no reason to believe that house number 20 will be larger than house number 1. The domain of an ordinal feature is a totally ordered set such as a set of characters or strings. Because ordinal features lack a linear scale, it does not make sense to add or subtract them; therefore, operations such as averaging ordinal features do not usually make sense or yield any information about the features. Similar to quantitative features in tree models, ordinal features result in a binary split. In general, ordinal features are not readily used in most geometric models. For example, linear models assume a Euclidian instance space where feature values are treated as Cartesian coordinates. For distance-based models, we can use ordinal features if we encode them as integers and the distance between them is simply their difference. This is sometimes referred to as the **hamming distance**.

Categorical features

Categorical features, sometimes called **nominal features**, do not have any ordering or scale, and therefore, they do not allow any statistical summary apart from the mode indicating the most frequent occurrence of a value. Categorical features are often best handled by probabilistic models; however, they can also be used in distance-based models using the hamming distance and by setting the distance to 0 for equal values and 1 for unequal values. A subtype of categorical features is the **Boolean feature,** which maps into the Boolean values of true or false.

Operations and statistics

Features can be defined by the allowable operations that can be performed on them. Consider two features: a person's age and their phone number. Although both these features can be described by integers, they actually represent two very different types of information. This is clear when we see which operations we can usefully perform on them. For example, calculating the average age of a group of people will give us a meaningful result; calculating the average phone number will not.

We can call the range of possible calculations that can be performed on a feature as its statistics. These statistics describe three separate aspects of data. These are – its **central tendency**, its **dispersion**, and its **shape**.

To calculate the central tendency of data, we usually use one or more of the following statistics: the mean (or average), the median (or the middle value in an ordered list), and the mode (or the majority of all values). The mode is the only statistic that can be applied to all data types. To calculate the median, we need feature values that can be somehow ordered, that is ordinal or quantitative. To calculate the mean, values must be expressed on some scale, such as the linear scale. In other words they will need to be quantitative features.

The most common way of calculating dispersion is through the statistics of variance or standard deviation. These are both really the same measure but on different scales, with standard deviation being useful because it is expressed on the same scale as the feature itself. Also, remember that the absolute difference between the mean and the median is never larger than the standard deviation. A simpler statistic for measuring dispersion is the range, which is just the difference between the minimum and maximum values. From here, of course, we can estimate the feature's central tendency by calculating the mid-range point. Another way to measure dispersion is using units such as percentiles or deciles to measure the ratio of instances falling below a particular value. For example, the pth percentile is the value that p percent of instances fall below.

Measuring shape statistics is a little more complicated and can be understood using the idea of the **central moment** of a sample. This is defined as follows:

$$m_k = \frac{1}{n}\sum_{i=1}^{n}(x_i - \mu)^k$$

Here, n is the number of samples, μ is the sample mean, and k is an integer. When $k = 1$, the first central moment is 0 because this is simply the average deviation from the mean, which is always 0. The second central moment is the average squared deviation from the mean, which is the variance. We can define **skewness** as follows:

$$\frac{m_3}{\sigma^3}$$

Here σ is the standard deviation. If this formula gives a value that is positive, then there are more instances with values above the mean rather than below. The data, when graphed, is skewed to the right. When the skew is negative, the converse is true.

We can define **kurtosis** as a similar relationship for the fourth central moment:

$$\frac{m_4}{\sigma^4}$$

It can be shown that a normal distribution has a kurtosis of 3. At values above this, the distribution will be more *peaked*. At kurtosis values below 3, the distribution will be *flatter*.

We previously discussed the three types of data, that is, categorical, ordinal, and quantitative.

Machine learning models will treat the different data types in very distinct ways. For example, a decision tree split on a categorical feature will give rise to as many children as there are values. For ordinal and quantitative features, the splits will be binary, with each parent giving rise to two children based on a threshold value. As a consequence, tree models treat quantitative features as ordinal, ignoring the features scale. When we consider probabilistic models such as the **Bayes classifier**, we can see that it actually treats ordinal features as categorical, and the only way in which it can handle quantitative features is to turn them into a finite number of discrete values, therefore converting them to categorical data.

Geometric models, in general, require features that are quantitative. For example, linear models operate in a Euclidean instance space, with the features acting as Cartesian coordinates. Each feature value is considered as a scalar relationship to other feature values. Distance-based models, such as the k-nearest neighbor, can incorporate categorical features by setting the distance to 0 for equal values and 1 for unequal values. Similarly, we can incorporate ordinal features into distance-based models by counting the number of values between two values. If we are encoding feature values as integers, then the distance is simply the numerical difference. By choosing an appropriate distance metric, it is possible to incorporate ordinal and categorical features into distance-based models.

Structured features

We assume that each instance can be represented as a vector of feature values and that all relevant aspects are represented by this vector. This is sometimes called an **abstraction** because we filter out unnecessary information and represent a real-world phenomena with a vector. For example, representing the entire works of Leo Tolstoy as a vector of word frequencies is an abstraction. We make no pretense that this abstraction will serve any more than a very particular limited application. We may learn something about Tolstoy's use of language and perhaps elicit some information regarding the sentiment and subject of Tolstoy's writing. However, we are unlikely to gain any significant insights into the broad canvas of the 19th century Russia portrayed in these works. A human reader, or a more sophisticated algorithm, will gain these insights not from the counting of each word but by the structure that these words are part of.

We can think of structured features in a similar way to how we may think about queries in a database programming language, such as SQL. A SQL query can represent an aggregation over variables to do things such as finding a particular phrase or finding all the passages involving a particular character. What we are doing in a machine learning context is creating another feature with these aggregate properties.

Structured features can be created prior to building the model or as part of the model itself. In the first case, the process can be understood as being a translation from the first order logic to a propositional logic. A problem with this approach is that it can create an explosion in the number of potential features as a result of combinations with existing features. Another important point is that, in the same way that in SQL one clause can cover a subset of another clause, structural features can also be logically related. This is exploited in the branch of machine learning that is particularly well suited to natural language processing, known as **inductive logic programming**.

Transforming features

When we transform features, our aim, obviously, is to make them more useful to our models. This can be done by adding, removing, or changing information represented by the feature. A common feature transformation is that of changing the feature type. A typical example is **binarization**, that is, transforming a categorical feature into a set of binary ones. Another example is changing an ordinal feature into a categorical feature. In both these cases, we lose information. In the first instance, the value of a single categorical feature is mutually exclusive, and this is not conveyed by the binary representation. In the second instance, we lose the ordering information. These types of transformations can be considered inductive because they consist of a well-defined logical procedure that does not involve an objective choice apart from the decision to carry out these transformations in the first place.

Binarization can be easily carried out using the `sklearn.preprocessing.`
`Binarizer` module. Let's take a look at the following commands:

```
from sklearn.preprocessing import Binarizer
from random import randint
bin=Binarizer(5)
X=[randint(0,10) for b in range(1,10)]
print(X)
print(bin.transform(X))
```

The following is the output for the preceding commands:

```
[5, 6, 1, 7, 5, 3, 3, 3, 7]
[[0 1 0 1 0 0 0 0 1]]
```

Features that are categorical often need to be encoded into integers. Consider a very simple dataset with just one categorical feature, City, with three possible values, Sydney, Perth, and Melbourne, and we decide to encode the three values as 0, 1, and 2, respectively. If this information is to be used in a linear classifier, then we write the constraint as a linear inequality with a weight parameter. The problem, however, is that this weight cannot encode for a three way choice. Suppose we have two classes, east coast and west coast, and we need our model to come up with a decision function that will reflect the fact that Perth is on the west coast and both Sydney and Melbourne are on the east coast. With a simple linear model, when the features are encoded in this way, then the decision function cannot come up with a rule that will put Sydney and Melbourne in the same class. The solution is to blow up the feature space to three features, each getting their own weights. This is called **one hot encoding**. Sciki-learn implements the `OneHotEncoder()` function to perform this task. This is an estimator that transforms each categorical feature, with m possible values into m binary features. Consider that we are using a model with data that consists of the city feature as described in the preceding example and two other features — gender, which can be either male or female, and an occupation, which can have three values — doctor, lawyer, or banker. So, for example, *a female banker from Sydney* would be represented as *[1,2,0]*. Three more samples are added for the following example:

```
from sklearn.preprocessing import OneHotEncoder
enc = OneHotEncoder()
enc.fit([[1,2,0], [1, 1, 0], [0, 2, 1], [1, 0, 2]])
print(enc.transform([1,2,0]).toarray())
```

We will get the following output:

$$\begin{bmatrix} [0.\ 1.\ 0.\ 0.\ 1.\ 1.\ 0.\ 0.] \end{bmatrix}$$

Since we have two genders, three cities, and three jobs in this dataset, the first two numbers in the transform array represent the gender, the next three represent the city, and the final three represent the occupation.

Discretization

I have already briefly mentioned the idea of thresholding in relation to decision trees, where we transform an ordinal or quantitative feature into a binary feature by finding an appropriate feature value to split on. There are a number of methods, both supervised and unsupervised, that can be used to find an appropriate split in continuous data, for example, using the statistics of central tendency (supervised), such as the mean or median or optimizing an objective function based on criteria such as information gain.

We can go further and create multiple thresholds, transforming a quantitative feature into an ordinal one. Here, we divide a continuous quantitative feature into numerous discrete ordinal values. Each of these values is referred to as a **bin**, and each bin represents an interval on the original quantitative feature. Many machine learning models require discrete values. It becomes easier and more comprehensible to create rule-based models using discrete values. Discretization also makes features more compact and may make our algorithms more efficient.

One of the most common approaches is to choose bins such that each bin has approximately the same number of instances. This is called **equal frequency discretization**, and if we apply it to just two bins, then this is the same as using the median as a threshold. This approach can be quite useful because the bin boundaries can be set up in such a way that they represent quantiles. For example, if we have 100 bins, then each bin represents a percentile.

Alternatively, we can choose the boundaries so that each bin has the same interval width. This is called **equal width discretization**. A way of working out the value of this bin's width interval is simply to divide the feature range by the number of bins. Sometimes, the features do not have an upper or lower limit, and we cannot calculate its range. In this case, integer numbers of standard deviations above and below the mean can be used. Both width and frequency discretization are unsupervised. They do not require any knowledge of the class labels to work.

Let's now turn our attention to supervised discretization. There are essentially two approaches: the top-down or **divisive**, and the **agglomerative** or bottom-up approach. As the names suggest, divisive works by initially assuming that all samples belong to the same bin and then progressively splits the bins. Agglomerative methods begin with a bin for each instance and progressively merges these bins. Both methods require some stopping criteria to decide if further splits are necessary.

The process of recursively partitioning feature values through thresholding is an example of divisive discretization. To make this work, we need a scoring function that finds the best threshold for particular feature values. A common way to do this is to calculate the information gain of the split or its entropy. By determining how many positive and negative samples are covered by a particular split, we can progressively split features based on this criterion.

Simple discretization operations can be carried out by the Pandas **cut** and **qcut** methods. Consider the following example:

```
import pandas as pd
import numpy as np
print(pd.cut(np.array([1,2,3,4]), 3, retbins = True, right = False))
```

Here is the output observed:

```
([[1, 2), [2, 3), [3, 4.003), [3, 4.003)]
Categories (3, object): [[1, 2) < [2, 3) < [3, 4.003)], array([ 1.   , 2.   ,
3.   , 4.003]))
```

Normalization

Thresholding and discretization, both, remove the scale of a quantitative feature and, depending on the application, this may not be what we want. Alternatively, we may want to add a measure of scale to ordinal or categorical features. In an unsupervised setting, we refer to this as **normalization**. This is often used to deal with quantitative features that have been measured on a different scale. Feature values that approximate a normal distribution can be converted to *z* scores. This is simply a signed number of standard deviations above or below the mean. A positive *z* score indicates a number of standard deviations above the mean, and a negative *z* score indicates the number of standard deviations below the mean. For some features, it may be more convenient to use the variance rather than the standard deviation.

A stricter form of normalization expresses a feature on a 0 to 1 scale. If we know a features range, we can simply use a linear scaling, that is, divide the difference between the original feature value and the lowest value with the difference between the lowest and highest value. This is expressed in the following:

$$f_n = \frac{(f-l)}{(h-l)}$$

Here, f_n is the normalized feature, f is the original feature, and l and h are the lowest and highest values, respectively. In many cases, we may have to guess the range. If we know something about a particular distribution, for example, in a normal distribution more than 99% of values are likely to fall within +3 or -3 standard deviations of the mean, then we can write a linear scaling such as the following:

$$f_n = \frac{(f-\mu)}{(6\sigma)} + \frac{1}{2}$$

Here, μ is the mean and σ is the standard deviation.

Calibration

Sometimes, we need to add scale information to an ordinal or categorical feature. This is called feature **calibration**. It is a supervised feature transformation that has a number of important applications. For example, it allows models that require scaled features, such as linear classifiers, to handle categorical and ordinal data. It also gives models the flexibility to treat features as ordinal, categorical, or quantitative. For binary classification, we can use the posterior probability of the positive class, given a features value, to calculate the scale. For many probabilistic models, such as naive Bayes, this method of calibration has the added advantage in that the model does not require any additional training once the features are calibrated. For categorical features, we can determine these probabilities by simply collecting the relative frequencies from a training set.

There are cases where we might need to turn quantitative or ordinal features in to categorical features yet maintain an ordering. One of the main ways we do this is through a process of **logistic calibration**. If we assume that the feature is normally distributed with the same variance, then it turns out that we can express a likelihood ratio, the ration of positive and negative classes, given a feature value v, as follows:

$$LR(v) = \frac{(P(v|pos))}{(P(v|neg))} = exp(d'z)$$

Where d prime is the difference between the means of the two classes divided by the standard deviation:

$$d' = \frac{(\mu pos - \mu neg)}{(\sigma)}$$

Also, z is the z score:

$$\frac{(v-\mu)}{\sigma} \text{ assuming equal class distribution} : \mu = \frac{(\mu pos + \mu neg)}{2}$$

To neutralize the effect of nonuniform class distributions, we can calculate calibrated features using the following:

$$F_c(x) = \frac{(LRF(x))}{(1 + LR(F(x)))} = exp \frac{(d'z(x))}{(1 + exp(d'z(x)))}$$

This, you may notice, is exactly the sigmoid activation function we used for logistic regression. To summarize logistic calibration, we essentially use three steps:

1. Estimate the class means for the positive and negative classes.
2. Transform the features into z scores.
3. Apply the sigmoid function to give calibrated probabilities.

Sometimes, we may skip the last step, specifically if we are using distance-based models where we expect the scale to be additive in order to calculate Euclidian distance. You may notice that our final calibrated features are multiplicative in scale.

Another calibration technique, **isotonic calibration**, is used on both quantitative and ordinal features. This uses what is known as a **ROC** curve (stands for **Receiver Operator Characteristic**) similar to the coverage maps used in the discussion of logical models in *Chapter 4, Models – Learning from Information*. The difference is that with an ROC curve, we normalize the axis to *[0,1]*.

We can use the `sklearn` package to create an ROC curve:

```
import matplotlib.pyplot as plt
from sklearn import svm, datasets
from sklearn.metrics import roc_curve, auc
from sklearn.cross_validation import train_test_split
from sklearn.preprocessing import label_binarize
from sklearn.multiclass import OneVsRestClassifier


X, y = datasets.make_classification(n_samples=100,n_classes=3,n_
features=5, n_informative=3, n_redundant=0,random_state=42)
# Binarize the output
y = label_binarize(y, classes=[0, 1, 2])
n_classes = y.shape[1]
X_train, X_test, y_train, y_test = train_test_split(X, y, test_size=.5)
classifier = OneVsRestClassifier(svm.SVC(kernel='linear',
probability=True, ))
y_score = classifier.fit(X_train, y_train).decision_function(X_test)
fpr, tpr, _ = roc_curve(y_test[:,0], y_score[:,0])
roc_auc = auc(fpr, tpr)
plt.figure()
plt.plot(fpr, tpr, label='ROC AUC %0.2f' % roc_auc)
plt.plot([0, 1], [0, 1], 'k--')
plt.xlim([0.0, 1.0])
plt.ylim([0.0, 1.05])
plt.xlabel('False Positive Rate')
plt.ylabel('True Positive Rate')
plt.title('Receiver operating characteristic')
plt.legend(loc="best")
plt.show()
```

Here is the output observed:

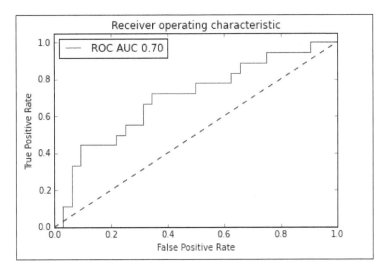

The ROC curve maps the true positive rates against the false positive rate for different threshold values. In the preceding diagram, this is represented by the dotted line. Once we have constructed the ROC curve, we calculate the number of positives, m_i, and the total number of instances, n_i, in each segment of the convex hull. The following formula is then used to calculate the calibrated feature values:

$$v_c = \frac{\left(m_i + 1\right)}{\left(m_i + 1 + c\left(n_i - m_i + 1\right)\right)}$$

In this formula, c is the prior odds, that is, the ratio of the probability of the positive class over the probability of the negative class.

So far in our discussion on feature transformations, we assumed that we know all the values for every feature. In the real world, this is often not the case. If we are working with probabilistic models, we can estimate the value of a missing feature by taking a weighted average over all features values. An important consideration is that the existence of missing feature values may be correlated with the target variable. For example, data in an individual's medical history is a reflection of the types of testing that are performed, and this in turn is related to an assessment on risk factors for certain diseases.

If we are using a tree model, we can randomly choose a missing value, allowing the model to split on it. This, however, will not work for linear models. In this case, we need to fill in the missing values through a process of **imputation**. For classification, we can simply use the statistics of the mean, median, and mode over the observed features to impute the missing values. If we want to take feature correlation into account, we can construct a predictive model for each incomplete feature to predict missing values.

Since scikit-learn estimators always assume that all values in an array are numeric, missing values, either encoded as blanks, NaN, or other placeholders, will generate errors. Also, since we may not want to discard entire rows or columns, as these may contain valuable information, we need to use an imputation strategy to complete the dataset. In the following code snippet, we will use the `Imputer` class:

```
from sklearn.preprocessing import Binarizer, Imputer, OneHotEncoder
imp = Imputer(missing_values='NaN', strategy='mean', axis=0)
print(imp.fit_transform([[1, 3], [4, np.nan], [5, 6]]))
```

Here is the output:

```
[[ 1.    3. ]
 [ 4.    4.5]
 [ 5.    6. ]]
```

Many machine learning algorithms require that features are **standardized**. This means that they will work best when the individual features look more or less like normally distributed data with near-zero mean and unit variance. The easiest way to do this is by subtracting the mean value from each feature and scaling it by dividing by the standard deviation. This can be achieved by the `scale()` function or the `standardScaler()` function in the `sklearn.preprocessing()` function. Although these functions will accept sparse data, they probably should not be used in such situations because centering sparse data would likely destroy its structure. It is recommended to use the `MacAbsScaler()` or `maxabs_scale()` function in these cases. The former scales and translates each feature individually by its maximum absolute value. The latter scales each feature individually to a range of *[-1,1]*. Another specific case is when we have outliers in the data. In these cases using the `robust_scale()` or `RobustScaler()` function is recommended.

Often, we may want to add complexity to a model by adding polynomial terms. This can be done using the `PolynomialFeatures()` function:

```
from sklearn.preprocessing import PolynomialFeatures
X=np.arange(9).reshape(3,3)
```

```
poly=PolynomialFeatures(degree=2)
print(X)
print(poly.fit_transform(X))
```

We will observe the following output:

$$\begin{bmatrix} [0 & 1 & 2] \\ [3 & 4 & 5] \\ [6 & 7 & 8] \end{bmatrix}$$

$$\begin{bmatrix} [1 & 0 & 1 & 2 & 0 & 0 & 0 & 1 & 2 & 4] \\ [1 & 3 & 4 & 5 & 9 & 12 & 15 & 16 & 20 & 25] \\ [1 & 6 & 7 & 8 & 36 & 42 & 48 & 49 & 56 & 64] \end{bmatrix}$$

Principle component analysis

Principle Component Analysis (PCA) is the most common form of dimensionality reduction that we can apply to features. Consider the example of a dataset consisting of two features and we would like to convert this two-dimensional data into one dimension. A natural approach would be to draw a line of the closest fit and project each data point onto this line, as shown in the following graph:

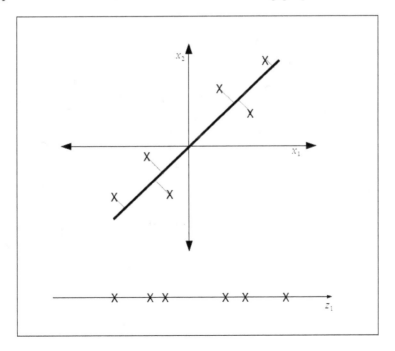

PCA attempts to find a surface to project the data by minimizing the distance between the data points and the line we are attempting to project this data to. For the more general case where we have *n* dimensions and we want to reduce this space to k-dimensions, we find *k* vectors *u(1),u(2), ..., u(k)* onto which to project the data so as to minimize the projection error. That is we are trying to find a k-dimensional surface to project the data.

This looks superficially like linear regression however it is different in several important ways. With linear regression we are trying to predict the value of some output variable given an input variable. In PCA we are not trying to predict an output variable, rather we are trying to find a subspace onto which to project our input data. The error distances, as represented in the preceding graph, is not the vertical distance between a point and the line, as is the case for linear regression, but rather the closest orthogonal distance between the point and the line. Thus, the error lines are at an angle to the axis and form a right angle with our projection line.

An important point is that in most cases, PCA requires that the features are scaled and are mean normalized, that is, the features have zero mean and have a comparable range of values. We can calculate the mean using the following formula:

$$\mu_j = \frac{1}{m} \sum_{i=1}^{m} x_j^{(i)}$$

The sum is calculated by replacing the following:

$$x_j^{(i)} \text{ with } x_j - \mu_j$$

If the features have scales that are significantly different, we can rescale using the following:

$$\frac{\left(x_j - \mu_j\right)}{\sigma_j}$$

These functions are available in the `sklearn.preprocessing` module.

The mathematical process of calculating both the lower dimensional vectors and the points on these vectors where we project our original data involve first calculating the covariance matrix and then calculating the eigenvectors of this matrix. To calculate these values from first principles is quite a complicated process. Fortunately, the `sklearn` package has a library for doing just this:

```
from sklearn.decomposition import PCA
import numpy as np
X = np.array([[-1, -1], [-2, -1], [-3, -2], [1, 1], [2, 1], [3, 2]])
pca = PCA(n_components=1)
pca.fit(X)
print(pca.transform(X))
```

We will get the following output:

$$\begin{bmatrix} [-1.3834058] \\ [-2.22189802] \\ [-3.60530382] \\ [1.3834058 \quad] \\ [2.22189802 \quad] \\ [3.60530382 \quad] \end{bmatrix}$$

Summary

There are a rich variety of ways in which we can both transform and construct new features to make our models work more efficiently and give more accurate results. In general, there are no hard and fast rules for deciding which of the methods to use for a particular model. Much depends on the feature types (quantitative, ordinal, or categorical) that you are working with. A good first approach is to normalize and scale the features, and if the model requires it, transform the feature to an appropriate type, as we do through discretization. If the model performs poorly, it may be necessary to apply further preprocessing such as PCA. In the next chapter, we will look at ways in which we can combine different types of models, through the use of ensembles, to improve performance and provide greater predictive power.

8
Learning with Ensembles

The motivation for creating machine learning ensembles comes from clear intuitions and is grounded in a rich theoretical history. Diversity, in many natural and human-made systems, makes them more resilient to perturbations. Similarly, we have seen that averaging results from a number of measurements can often result in a more stable models that are less susceptible to random fluctuations, such as outliers or errors in data collection.

In this chapter, we will divide this rather large and diverse space into the following topics:

- Ensemble types
- Bagging
- Random forests
- Boosting

Ensemble types

Ensemble techniques can be broadly divided into two types:

- **Averaging method**: This is the method in which several estimators are run independently and their predictions are averaged. This includes random forests and bagging methods.

- **Boosting method**: This is the method in which weak learners are built sequentially using weighted distributions of the data based on the error rates.

Ensemble methods use multiple models to obtain better performance than any single constituent model. The aim is to not only build diverse and robust models, but also work within limitations, such as processing speed and return times. When working with large datasets and quick response times, this can be a significant developmental bottleneck. Troubleshooting and diagnostics are an important aspect of working with all machine learning models, but especially when we are dealing with models that may take days to run.

The types of machine learning ensembles that can be created are as diverse as the models themselves, and the main considerations revolve around three things: how we divide our data, how we select the models, and the methods we use to combine their results. This simplistic statement actually encompasses a very large and diverse space.

Bagging

Bagging, also called **bootstrap aggregating**, comes in a few flavors and these are defined by the way they draw random subsets from the training data. Most commonly, bagging refers to drawing samples with replacement. Because the samples are replaced, it is possible for the generated datasets to contain duplicates. It also means that data points may be excluded from a particular generated dataset, even if this generated set is the same size as the original. Each of the generated datasets will be different and this is a way to create diversity among the models in an ensemble. We can calculate the probability that a data point is not selected in a sample using the following example:

$$\left(1 - \frac{1}{n}\right)^n$$

Here, n is the number of bootstrap samples. Each of the n bootstrap samples results in a different hypothesis. The class is predicted either by averaging the models or by choosing the class predicted by the majority of models. Consider an ensemble of linear classifiers. If we use majority voting to determine the predicted class, we create a piece-wise linear classifier boundary. If we transform the votes to probabilities, then we partition the instance space into segments that can each potentially have a different score.

It should also be mentioned that it is possible, and sometimes desirable, to use random subsets of features; this is called **subspace sampling**. Bagging estimators work best with complex models such as fully developed decision trees because they can help reduce overfitting. They provide a simple, out-of-the-box, way to improve a single model.

Scikit-learn implements a `BaggingClassifier` and `BaggingRegressor` objects. Here are some of their most important parameters:

Parameter	Type	Description	Default
base_estimator	Estimator	This is the model the ensemble is built on.	Decision tree
n_estimators	Int	This is the number of base estimators.	10
max_samples	Int or float	This is the number of samples to draw. If float draw max_samples*X.shape[0].	1.0
max_features	Int or float	This is the number of features to draw. If float draw max_features*X.shape[1].	1.0
bootstrap	Boolean	These are the samples drawn with replacement.	True
bootstrap_features	Boolean	These are the features drawn with replacement.	False

As an example, the following snippet instantiates a bagging classifier comprising of 50 decision tree classifier base estimators each built on random subsets of half the features and half the samples:

```
from sklearn.ensemble import BaggingClassifier

from sklearn.tree import DecisionTreeClassifier

from sklearn import datasets


bcls=BaggingClassifier(DecisionTreeClassifier(),max_samples=0.5, max_
features=0.5, n_estimators=50)

X,y=datasets.make_blobs(n_samples=8000,centers=2, random_state=0,
cluster_std=4)

bcls.fit(X,y)

print(bcls.score(X,y))
```

Random forests

Tree-based models are particularly well suited to ensembles, primarily because they can be sensitive to changes in the training data. Tree models can be very effective when used with **subspace sampling**, resulting in more diverse models and, since each model in the ensemble is working on only a subset of the features, it reduces the training time. This builds each tree using a different random subset of the features and is therefore called a **random forest**.

A random forest partitions an instance space by finding the intersection of the partitions in the individual trees in the forest. It defines a partition that can be finer, that is, will take in more detail, than a partition created by any individual tree in the forest. In principle, a random forest can be mapped back to an individual tree, since each intersection corresponds to combining the branches of two different trees. The random forest can be thought of as essentially an alternative training algorithm for tree-based models. A linear classifier in a bagging ensemble is able to learn a complicated decision boundary that would be impossible for a single linear classifier to learn.

The `sklearn.ensemble` module has two algorithms based on decision trees, random forests and extremely randomized trees. They both create diverse classifiers by introducing randomness into their construction and both include classes for classification and regression. With the `RandomForestClassifier` and `RandomForestRegressor` class each tree is built using bootstrap samples. The split chosen by the model is not the best split among all features, but is chosen from a random subset of features.

Extra trees

The `extra trees` method, as with random forests, uses a random subset of features, but instead of using the most discriminative thresholds, the best of a randomly generated set of thresholds is used. This acts to reduce variance at the expense of a small increase in bias. The two classes are `ExtraTreesClassifier` and `ExtraTreesRegressor`.

Let's take a look at an example of the `random forest` classifier and the `extra trees` classifier. In this example, we use `VotingClassifier` to combine different classifiers. The voting classifier can help balance out an individual model's weakness. In this example, we pass four weights to the function. These weights determine each individual model's contribution to the overall result. We can see that the two tree models overfit the training data, but also tend to perform better on the test data. We can also see that `ExtraTreesClassifier` achieved slightly better results on the test set compared to the `RandomForest` object. Also, the `VotingClasifier` object performed better on the test set than all its constituent classifiers. It is worth, while running this with different weightings as well as on different datasets, seeing how the performance of each model changes:

```
from sklearn import cross_validation
import numpy as np
import matplotlib.pyplot as plt
from sklearn.linear_model import LogisticRegression
from sklearn.naive_bayes import GaussianNB
```

```
from sklearn.ensemble import RandomForestClassifier
from sklearn.ensemble import ExtraTreesClassifier
from sklearn.ensemble import VotingClassifier
from sklearn import datasets


def vclas(w1,w2,w3, w4):


    X , y = datasets.make_classification(n_features= 10, n_informative=4,
n_samples=500, n_clusters_per_class=5)
    Xtrain,Xtest, ytrain,ytest= cross_validation.train_test_
split(X,y,test_size=0.4)


    clf1 = LogisticRegression(random_state=123)
    clf2 = GaussianNB()
    clf3 = RandomForestClassifier(n_estimators=10,bootstrap=True, random_
state=123)
    clf4= ExtraTreesClassifier(n_estimators=10, bootstrap=True,random_
state=123)


    clfes=[clf1,clf2,clf3,clf4]


    eclf = VotingClassifier(estimators=[('lr', clf1), ('gnb', clf2),
('rf', clf3),('et',clf4)],
                            voting='soft',
                            weights=[w1, w2, w3,w4])



    [c.fit(Xtrain, ytrain) for c in (clf1, clf2, clf3,clf4, eclf)]


    N = 5
    ind = np.arange(N)
    width = 0.3
    fig, ax = plt.subplots()


    for i, clf in enumerate(clfes):
        print(clf,i)
```

```
        p1=ax.bar(i,clfes[i].score(Xtrain,ytrain,),
width=width,color="black")

        p2=ax.bar(i+width,clfes[i].score(Xtest,ytest,),
width=width,color="grey")

    ax.bar(len(clfes)+width,eclf.score(Xtrain,ytrain,),
width=width,color="black")

    ax.bar(len(clfes)+width *2,eclf.score(Xtest,ytest,),
width=width,color="grey")

    plt.axvline(3.8, color='k', linestyle='dashed')

    ax.set_xticks(ind + width)

    ax.set_xticklabels(['LogisticRegression',

                    'GaussianNB',

                    'RandomForestClassifier',

                    'ExtraTrees',

                    'VotingClassifier'],

                   rotation=40,

                   ha='right')

    plt.title('Training and test score for different classifiers')

    plt.legend([p1[0], p2[0]], ['training', 'test'], loc='lower left')

    plt.show()
```

```
vclas(1,3,5,4)
```

You will observe the following output:

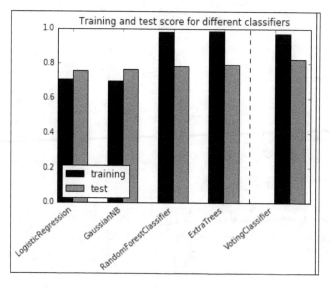

Tree models allow us to assess the relative rank of features in terms of the expected fraction of samples they contribute to. Here, we use one to evaluate the importance of each features in a classification task. A feature's relative importance is based on where it is represented in the tree. Features at the top of a tree contribute to the final decision of a larger proportion of input samples.

The following example uses an ExtraTreesClassifier class to map feature importance. The dataset we are using consists of 10 images, each of 40 people, which is 400 images in total. Each image has a label indicating the person's identity. In this task, each pixel is a feature; in the output, the pixel's brightness represents the feature's relative importance. The brighter the pixel, the more important the features. Note that in this model, the brightest pixels are in the forehead region and we should be careful how we interpret this. Since most photographs are illuminated from above the head, the apparently high importance of these pixels may be due to the fact that foreheads tend to be better illuminated, and therefore reveal more detail about an individual, rather than the intrinsic properties of a person's forehead in indicating their identity:

```
import matplotlib.pyplot as plt

from sklearn.datasets import fetch_olivetti_faces

from sklearn.ensemble import ExtraTreesClassifier

data = fetch_olivetti_faces()

def importance(n_estimators=500, max_features=128, n_jobs=3, random_
state=0):

    X = data.images.reshape((len(data.images), -1))

    y = data.target

    forest = ExtraTreesClassifier(n_estimators,max_features=max_features,
n_jobs=n_jobs, random_state=random_state)

    forest.fit(X, y)

    dstring=" cores=%d..." % n_jobs + " features=%s..." % max_features
+"estimators=%d..." %n_estimators + "random=%d" %random_state

    print(dstring)

    importances = forest.feature_importances_

    importances = importances.reshape(data.images[0].shape)

    plt.matshow(importances, cmap=plt.cm.hot)

    plt.title(dstring)

    #plt.savefig('etreesImportance'+ dstring + '.png')

    plt.show()


importance()
```

The output for the preceding code is as follows:

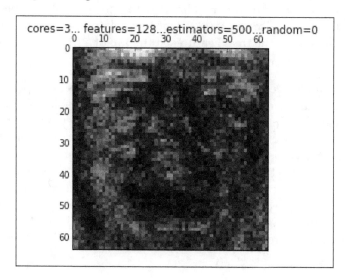

Boosting

Earlier in this book, I introduced the idea of the PAC learning model and the idea of concept classes. A related idea is that of **weak learnability**. Here each of the learning algorithms in the ensemble need only perform slightly better than chance. For example if each algorithm in the ensemble is correct at least 51% of the time then the criteria of weak learnability are satisfied. It turns out that the ideas of PAC and weak learnability are essentially the same except that for the latter, we drop the requirement that the algorithm must achieve arbitrarily high accuracy. However, it merely performs better than a random hypothesis. How is this useful, you may ask? It is often easier to find rough *rules of thumb* rather than a highly accurate prediction rule. This weak learning model may only perform slightly better than chance; however, if we *boost* this learner by running it many times on different weighted distributions of the data and by combining these learners, we can, hopefully, build a single prediction rule that performs much better than any of the individual weak learning rules.

Boosting is a simple and powerful idea. It extends bagging by taking into account a model's training error. For example, if we train a linear classifier and find that it misclassified a certain set of instances. If we train a subsequent model on a dataset containing duplicates of these misclassified instances, then we would expect that this newly trained model would perform better on a test set. By including duplicates of misclassified instances in the training set, we are shifting the mean of the data set towards these instances. This forces the learner to focus on the most difficult-to-classify examples. This is achieved in practice by giving misclassified instances higher weight and then modifying the model to take this in to account, for example, in a linear classifier we can calculate the class means by using weighted averages.

Starting from a dataset of uniform weights that sum to one, we run the classifier and will likely misclassify some instances. To boost the weight of these instances, we assign them half the total weight. For example, consider a classifier that gives us the following results:

	Predicted positive	Predicted negative	Total
Actual pos.	24	16	40
Actual neg.	9	51	60
Totals	33	67	100

The error rate is $\varepsilon = (9 + 16)/100 = 0.25$.

We want to assign half the error weight to the misclassified samples, and since we started with uniform weights that sum to 1, the current weight assigned to the misclassified examples is simply the error rate. To update the weights, therefore, we multiply them by the factor $1/2\varepsilon$. Assuming that the error rate is less than 0.5, this results in an increase in the weights of the misclassified examples. To ensure that the weights still sum to 1, we multiply the correctly classified examples by $\frac{1}{2}(1-\varepsilon)$. In this example, the error rate, the initial weights of the incorrectly classified samples, is .25 and we want it to be .5, that is, half the total weights, so we multiply this initial error rate by 2. The weights for the correctly classified instances are $1/2(1-\varepsilon) = 2/3$. Taking these weights into account results into the following table:

	Predicted positive	Predicted negative	Total
Actual pos.	16	32	48
Actual neg.	18	34	60
Total	33	67	100

The final piece we need is a confidence factor, *a*, which is applied to each model in the ensemble. This is used to make an ensemble prediction based on the weighted averages from each individual model. We want this to increase with decreasing errors. A common way to ensure this happens is to set the confidence factor to the following:

$$\alpha_t = ln\sqrt{\left(\frac{\left(1-\epsilon_t\right)}{\epsilon_t}\right)}$$

So we are given a dataset, such as following:

$$\left(x_1 y_1\right),\ldots,\left(x_m y_m\right) where\ x_i \in X, y_i \in Y = \{-1,+1\}$$

We then initialize an equal weighted distribution, such as the following:

$$W_1\left(i\right) = \frac{1}{m}$$

Using a weak classifier, h_t, we can write an updated rule as follows:

$$W_{(t+1)}\left(i\right) = \frac{\left(W_t\left(i\right)exp\left(-\alpha_t y_i h_t\left(x_i\right)\right)\right)}{Z_t}$$

With the normalization factor, such as the following:

$$Z_t = \sum_{i=1}^{m}\left(W_t\left(i\right)exp\left(-\alpha_t y_i h_t\left(x_i\right)\right)\right)$$

Note that $exp(-y_i h_t(x_i))$ is positive and greater than 1 if $-y_i h_t(x_i)$ is positive, and this happens if x_i is misclassified. The result is that the update rule will increase the weight of a misclassified example and decrease the weight of correctly classified samples.

We can write the final classifier as follows:

$$H(x) = sign\left(\sum_{t=1}^{T} \alpha h_t(x)\right)$$

Adaboost

One of the most popular boosting algorithms is called **AdaBoost** or **adaptive boosting**. Here, a decision tree classifier is used as the base learner and it builds a decision boundary on data that is not linearly separable:

```python
import numpy as np
import matplotlib.pyplot as plt
from sklearn.ensemble import AdaBoostClassifier
from sklearn.tree import DecisionTreeClassifier
from sklearn.datasets import make_blobs


plot_colors = "br"
plot_step = 0.02
class_names = "AB"
tree= DecisionTreeClassifier()
boost=AdaBoostClassifier()
X,y=make_blobs(n_samples=500,centers=2, random_state=0, cluster_std=2)
boost.fit(X,y)
plt.figure(figsize=(10, 5))


# Plot the decision boundaries
plt.subplot(121)
x_min, x_max = X[:, 0].min() - 1, X[:, 0].max() + 1
y_min, y_max = X[:, 1].min() - 1, X[:, 1].max() + 1
xx, yy = np.meshgrid(np.arange(x_min, x_max, plot_step),
                     np.arange(y_min, y_max, plot_step))


Z = boost.predict(np.c_[xx.ravel(), yy.ravel()])
Z = Z.reshape(xx.shape)
```

```
cs = plt.contourf(xx, yy, Z, cmap=plt.cm.Paired)
plt.axis("tight")


for i, n, c in zip(range(2), class_names, plot_colors):
    idx = np.where(y == i)
    plt.scatter(X[idx, 0], X[idx, 1],
                c=c, cmap=plt.cm.Paired,
                label="Class %s" % n)
plt.title('Decision Boundary')

twoclass_output = boost.decision_function(X)
plot_range = (twoclass_output.min(), twoclass_output.max())
plt.subplot(122)
for i, n, c in zip(range(2), class_names, plot_colors):
    plt.hist(twoclass_output[y == i],
             bins=20,
             range=plot_range,
             facecolor=c,
             label='Class %s' % n,
             alpha=.5)
x1, x2, y1, y2 = plt.axis()
plt.axis((x1, x2, y1, y2))
plt.legend(loc='upper left')
plt.ylabel('Samples')
plt.xlabel('Score')
plt.title('Decision Scores')
plt.show()
print("Mean Accuracy =%f" % boost.score(X,y))
```

The following is the output of the preceding commands:

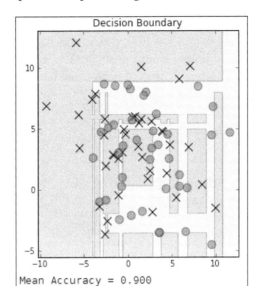

Gradient boosting

Gradient tree boosting is a very useful algorithm for both regression and classification problems. One of its major advantages is that it naturally handles mixed data types, and it is also quite robust to outliers. Additionally, it has better predictive powers than many other algorithms; however, its sequential architecture makes it unsuitable for parallel techniques, and therefore, it does not scale well to large data sets. For datasets with a large number of classes, it is recommended to use `RandomForestClassifier` instead. Gradient boosting typically uses decision trees to build a prediction model based on an ensemble of weak learners, applying an optimization algorithm on the cost function.

In the following example, we create a function that builds a gradient boosting classifier and graphs its cumulative loss versus the number of iterations. The `GradientBoostingClassifier` class has an `oob_improvement_` attribute and is used here calculate an estimate of the test loss on each iteration. This gives us a reduction in the loss compared to the previous iteration. This can be a very useful heuristic for determining the number of optimum iterations. Here, we plot the cumulative improvement of two gradient boosting classifiers. Each classifier is identical but for a different learning rate, *.01* in the case of the dotted line and *.001* for the solid line.

The learning rate shrinks the contribution of each tree, and this means that there is a tradeoff with the number of estimators. Here, we actually see that with a larger learning rate, the model appears to reach its optimum performance faster than the model with a lower learning rate. However, this models appears to achieve better results overall. What usually occurs in practice is that `oob_improvement` deviates in a pessimistic way over a large number of iterations. Let's take a look at the following commands:

```python
import numpy as np
import matplotlib.pyplot as plt
from sklearn import ensemble
from sklearn.cross_validation import train_test_split
from sklearn import datasets


def gbt(params, X,y,ls):
    clf = ensemble.GradientBoostingClassifier(**params)
    clf.fit(X_train, y_train)
    cumsum = np.cumsum(clf.oob_improvement_)
    n = np.arange(params['n_estimators'])
    oob_best_iter = n[np.argmax(cumsum)]
    plt.xlabel('Iterations')
    plt.ylabel('Improvement')
    plt.axvline(x=oob_best_iter,linestyle=ls)
    plt.plot(n, cumsum, linestyle=ls)


X,y=datasets.make_blobs(n_samples=50,centers=5, random_state=0, cluster_
std=5)
X_train, X_test, y_train, y_test = train_test_split(X, y, test_size=0.5,
random_state=9)


p1 = {'n_estimators': 1200, 'max_depth': 3, 'subsample': 0.5,
        'learning_rate': 0.01, 'min_samples_leaf': 1, 'random_state':
3}
p2 = {'n_estimators': 1200, 'max_depth': 3, 'subsample': 0.5,
        'learning_rate': 0.001, 'min_samples_leaf': 1, 'random_state':
3}


gbt(p1, X,y, ls='--')
gbt(p2, X,y, ls='-')
```

You will observe the following output:

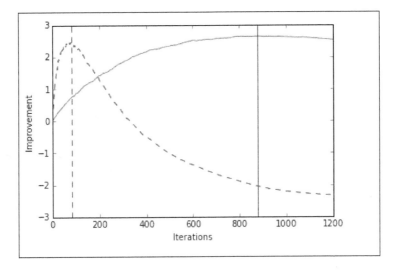

Ensemble strategies

We looked at two broad ensemble techniques: bagging, as applied random forests and extra trees, and boosting, in particular AdaBoost and gradient tree boosting. There are of course many other variants and combinations of these. In the last section of this chapter, I want to examine some strategies for choosing and applying different ensembles to particular tasks.

Generally, in classification tasks, there are three reasons why a model may misclassify a test instance. Firstly, it may simply be unavoidable if features from different classes are described by the same feature vectors. In probabilistic models, this happens when the class distributions overlap so that an instance has non-zero likelihoods for several classes. Here we can only approximate a target hypothesis.

The second reason for classification errors is that the model does not have the expressive capabilities to fully represent the target hypothesis. For example, even the best linear classifier will misclassify instances if the data is not linearly separable. This is due to the bias of the classifier. Although there is no single agreed way to measure bias, we can see that a nonlinear decision boundary will have less bias than a linear one, or that more complex decision boundaries will have less bias than simpler ones. We can also see that tree models have the least bias because they can continue to branch until only a single instance is covered by each leaf.

Now, it may seem that we should attempt to minimize bias; however, in most cases, lowering the bias tends to increase the variance and vice versa. Variance, as you have probably guessed, is the third source of classification errors. High variance models are highly dependent on training data. The nearest neighbor's classifier, for example, segments the instance space into single training points. If a training point near the decision boundary is moved, then that boundary will change. Tree models are also high variance, but for a different reason. Consider that we change the training data in such a way that a different feature is selected at the root of the tree. This will likely result in the rest of the tree being different.

A bagged ensemble of linear classifiers is able to learn a more complicated decision boundary through piecewise construction. Each classifier in the ensemble creates a segment of the decision boundary. This shows that bagging, indeed any ensemble method, is capable of reducing the bias of high bias models. However, what we find in practice is that boosting is generally a more effective way of reducing bias.

[Bagging is primarily a variance reduction technique and boosting is primarily a bias reduction technique.]

Bagging ensembles work most effectively with high variance models, such as complex trees, whereas boosting is typically used with high bias models such as linear classifiers.

We can look at boosting in terms of the **margin**. This can be understood as being the signed distance from the decision boundary; a positive sign indicates the correct class and a negative sign a false one. What can be shown is that boosting can increase this margin, even when samples are already on the correct side of the decision boundary. In other words, boosting can continue to improve performance on the test set even when the training error is zero.

Other methods

The major variations on ensemble methods are achieved by changing the way predictions of the base models are combined. We can actually define this as a learning problem in itself, given that the predictions of a set of base classifiers as features learn a **meta-model** that best combines their predictions. Learning a linear meta-model is known as **stacking** or **stacked generalization**. Stacking uses a weighted combination of all learners and, in a classification task, a combiner algorithm such as logistic regression is used to make the final prediction. Unlike bagging or boosting, and like bucketing, stacking is often used with models of different types.

Typical stacking routines involve the following steps:

1. Split the training set into two disjointed sets.
2. Train several base learners on the first set.
3. Test the base learner on the second set.
4. Use the predictions from the previous step to train a higher level learner.

Note that the first three steps are identical to cross validation; however, rather than taking a winner-takes-all approach, the base learners are combined, possibly nonlinearly.

A variation on this theme is **bucketing**. Here, a selection algorithm is used to choose the best model for each problem. This can be done, for example, using a perception to pick the best model by giving a weight to the predictions of each model. With a large set of diverse models, some will take longer to train than others. A way to use this in an ensemble is to first use the fast but imprecise algorithms to choose which slower, but more accurate, algorithms will likely do best.

We can incorporate diversity using a heterogeneous set of base learners. This diversity comes from the different learning algorithms and not the data. This means that each model can use the same training set. Often, the base models consist of sets of the same type but with different hyper parameter settings.

Ensembles, in general, consist of a set of base models and a meta-model that are trained to find the best way to combine these base models. If we are using a weighted set of models and combining their output in some way, we assume that if a model has a weight close to zero, then it will have very little influence on the output. It is conceivable that a base classifier has a negative weight, and in this case, its prediction would be inverted, relative to the other base models. We can even go further and attempt to predict how well a base model is likely to perform even before we train it. This is sometimes called **meta-learning**. This involves, first, training a variety of models on a large collection of data and constructing a model that will help us answer questions such as which model is likely to outperform another model on a particular dataset, or does the data indicate that particular (meta) parameters are likely to work best?

Remember that no learning algorithm can outperform another when evaluated over the space of all possible problems, such as predicting the next number is a sequence if all possible sequences are likely. Of course, learning problems in the real world have nonuniform distributions, and this enables us to build prediction models on them. The important question in meta-learning is how to design the features on which the meta-model is built. They need to combine the relevant characteristics of both the trained model and the dataset. This must include aspects of the data beyond the number and type of features, and the number of samples.

Summary

In this chapter, we looked at the major ensemble methods and their implementations in scikit-learn. It is clear that there is a large space to work in and finding what techniques work best for different types of problems is the key challenge. We saw that the problems of bias and variance each have their own solution, and it is essential to understand the key indicators of each of these. Achieving good results usually involves much experimentation, and using some of the simple techniques described in this chapter, you can begin your journey into machine learning ensembles.

In the next and last chapter, we will introduce the most important topic—model selection and evaluation—and examine some real-world problems from different perspectives.

9
Design Strategies and Case Studies

With the possible exception of data **munging**, evaluating is probably what machine learning scientists spend most of their time doing. Staring at lists of numbers and graphs, watching hopefully as their models run, and trying earnestly to make sense of their output. Evaluation is a cyclical process; we run models, evaluate the results, and plug in new parameters, each time hoping that this will result in a performance gain. Our work becomes more enjoyable and productive as we increase the efficiency of each evaluation cycle, and there are some tools and techniques that can help us achieve this. This chapter will introduce some of these through the following topics:

- Evaluating model performance
- Model selection
- Real-world case studies.
- Machine learning design at a glance

Evaluating model performance

Measuring a model's performance is an important machine learning task, and there are many varied parameters and heuristics for doing this. The importance of defining a scoring strategy should not be underestimated, and in Sklearn, there are basically three approaches:

- **Estimator score**: This refers to using the estimator's inbuilt `score()` method, specific to each estimator
- **Scoring parameters**: This refers to cross-validation tools relying on an internal scoring strategy
- **Metric functions**: These are implemented in the metrics module

We have seen examples of the estimator `score()` method, for example, `clf.score()`. In the case of a linear classifier, the `score()` method returns the mean accuracy. It is a quick and easy way to gauge an individual estimator's performance. However, this method is usually insufficient in itself for a number of reasons.

If we remember, accuracy is the sum of the true positive and true negative cases divided by the number of samples. Using this as a measure would indicate that if we performed a test on a number of patients to see if they had a particular disease, simply predicting that every patient was disease free would likely give us a high accuracy. Obviously, this is not what we want.

A better way to measure performance is using by **precision, (P)** and **Recall, (R)**. If you remember from the table in *Chapter 4, Models – Learning from Information*, precision, or specificity, is the proportion of predicted positive instances that are correct, that is, *TP/(TP+FP)*. Recall, or sensitivity, is *TP/(TP+FN)*. The F-measure is defined as *2*R*P/ (R+P)*. These measures ignore the true negative rate, and so they are not making an evaluation on how well a model handles negative cases.

Rather than use the score method of the estimator, it often makes sense to use specific scoring parameters such as those provided by the `cross_val_score` object. This has a `cv` parameter that controls how the data is split. It is usually set as an int, and it determines how many random consecutive splits are made on the data. Each of these has a different split point. This parameter can also be set to an iterable of train and test splits, or an object that can be used as a cross validation generator.

Also important in `cross_val_score` is the scoring parameter. This is usually set by a string indicating a scoring strategy. For classification, the default is *accuracy*, and some common values are `f1`, `precision`, `recall`, as well as the micro-averaged, macro-averaged, and weighted versions of these. For regression estimators, the scoring values are `mean_absolute_error`, `mean_squared error`, `median_absolute_error`, and `r2`.

The following code estimates the performance of three models on a dataset using 10 consecutive splits. Here, we print out the mean of each score, using several measures, for each of the four models. In a real-world situation, we will probably need to preprocess our data in one or more ways, and it is important to apply these data transformations to our test set as well as the training set. To make this easier, we can use the `sklearn.pipeline` module. This sequentially applies a list of transforms and a final estimator, and it allows us to assemble several steps that can be cross-validated together. Here, we also use the `StandardScaler()` class to scale the data. Scaling is applied to the logistic regression model and the decision tree by using two pipelines:

```
from sklearn import cross_validation
from sklearn.tree import DecisionTreeClassifier
```

```python
from sklearn import svm
from sklearn.linear_model import LogisticRegression
from sklearn.datasets import samples_generator
from sklearn.preprocessing import LabelEncoder
from sklearn.preprocessing import StandardScaler
from sklearn.cross_validation import cross_val_score
from sklearn.pipeline import Pipeline
X, y = samples_generator.make_classification(n_samples=1000,n_
informative=5, n_redundant=0,random_state=42)
le=LabelEncoder()
y=le.fit_transform(y)
Xtrain, Xtest, ytrain, ytest = cross_validation.train_test_split(X, y,
test_size=0.5, random_state=1)
clf1=DecisionTreeClassifier(max_depth=2,criterion='gini').
fit(Xtrain,ytrain)
clf2= svm.SVC(kernel='linear', probability=True, random_state=0).
fit(Xtrain,ytrain)
clf3=LogisticRegression(penalty='12', C=0.001).fit(Xtrain,ytrain)
pipe1=Pipeline([['sc',StandardScaler()],['mod',clf1]])
mod_labels=['Decision Tree','SVM','Logistic Regression' ]
print('10 fold cross validation: \n')
for mod,label in zip([pipe1,clf2,clf3], mod_labels):
    #print(label)
    auc_scores= cross_val_score(estimator= mod, X=Xtrain, y=ytrain,
cv=10, scoring ='roc_auc')
    p_scores= cross_val_score(estimator= mod, X=Xtrain, y=ytrain, cv=10,
scoring ='precision_macro')
    r_scores= cross_val_score(estimator= mod, X=Xtrain, y=ytrain, cv=10,
scoring ='recall_macro')
    f_scores= cross_val_score(estimator= mod, X=Xtrain, y=ytrain, cv=10,
scoring ='f1_macro')

    print(label)
    print("auc scores %2f +/- %2f " % (auc_scores.mean(), auc_scores.
std()))
    print("precision %2f +/- %2f " % (p_scores.mean(), p_scores.std()))
    print("recall %2f +/- %2f ]" % (r_scores.mean(), r_scores.std()))
    print("f scores %2f +/- %2f " % (f_scores.mean(), f_scores.std()))
```

On execution, you will see the following output:

```
10 fold cross validation:

Decision Tree
auc scores 0.692144 +/- 0.056865
precision 0.706912 +/- 0.065688
recall 0.648131 +/- 0.043604 ]
f scores 0.628455 +/- 0.051711
SVM
auc scores 0.768374 +/- 0.038460
precision 0.709994 +/- 0.058011
recall 0.707064 +/- 0.056323 ]
f scores 0.703605 +/- 0.055579
Logistic Regression
auc scores 0.754150 +/- 0.048137
precision 0.688979 +/- 0.077614
recall 0.686077 +/- 0.076052 ]
f scores 0.682859 +/- 0.075356
```

There are several variations on these techniques, most commonly using what is known as **k-fold cross validation**. This uses what is sometimes referred to as the *leave one out* strategy. First, the model is trained using $k-1$ of the folds as training data. The remaining data is then used to compute the performance measure. This is repeated for each of the folds. The performance is calculated as an average of all the folds.

Sklearn implements this using the `cross_validation.KFold` object. The important parameters are a required `int`, indicating the total number of elements, and an `n_folds` parameter, defaulting to 3, to indicate the number of folds. It also takes optional `shuffle` and `random_state` parameters indicating whether to shuffle the data before splitting, and what method to use to generate the random state. The default `random_state` parameter is to use the NumPy random number generator.

In the following snippet, we use the `LassoCV` object. This is a linear model trained with L1 regularization. The optimization function for regularized linear regression, if you remember, includes a constant (alpha) that multiplies the L1 regularization term. The `LassoCV` object automatically sets this alpha value, and to see how effective this is, we can compare the selected alpha and the score on each of the k-folds:

```
import numpy as np

from sklearn import cross_validation, datasets, linear_model

X,y=datasets.make_blobs(n_samples=80,centers=2, random_state=0, cluster_
std=2)

alphas = np.logspace(-4, -.5, 30)

lasso_cv = linear_model.LassoCV(alphas=alphas)
```

```
k_fold = cross_validation.KFold(len(X), 5)
alphas = np.logspace(-4, -.5, 30)


for k, (train, test) in enumerate(k_fold):
    lasso_cv.fit(X[train], y[train])
    print("[fold {0}] alpha: {1:.5f}, score: {2:.5f}".
        format(k, lasso_cv.alpha_, lasso_cv.score(X[test], y[test])))
```

The output of the preceding commands is as follows:

```
[fold 0] alpha: 0.01964, score: 0.42157
[fold 1] alpha: 0.00853, score: 0.52112
[fold 2] alpha: 0.00010, score: 0.48277
[fold 3] alpha: 0.00010, score: 0.42657
[fold 4] alpha: 0.00489, score: 0.54747
```

Sometimes, it is necessary to preserve the percentages of the classes in each fold. This is done using **stratified cross validation**. It can be helpful when classes are unbalanced, that is, when there is a larger number of some classes and very few of others. Using the stratified cv object may help correct defects in models that might cause bias because a class is not represented in a fold in large enough numbers to make an accurate prediction. However, this may also cause an unwanted increase in variance.

In the following example, we use stratified cross validation to test how significant the classification score is. This is done by repeating the classification procedure after randomizing the labels. The p value is the percentage of runs by which the score is greater than the classification score obtained initially. This code snippet uses the cross_validation.permutation_test_score method that takes the estimator, data, and labels as parameters. Here, we print out the initial test score, the p value, and the score on each permutation:

```
import numpy as np

from sklearn import linear_model

from sklearn.cross_validation import StratifiedKFold, permutation_test_
score

from sklearn import datasets


X,y=datasets.make_classification(n_samples=100, n_features=5)

n_classes = np.unique(y).size

cls=linear_model.LogisticRegression()
```

```
cv = StratifiedKFold(y, 2)

score, permutation_scores, pvalue = permutation_test_score(cls, X, y,
scoring="f1", cv=cv, n_permutations=10, n_jobs=1)


print("Classification score %s (pvalue : %s)" % (score, pvalue))

print("Permutation scores %s" % (permutation_scores))
```

This gives the following output:

```
Classification score 0.968962585034 (pvalue : 0.0909090909091)
Permutation scores [ 0.36310273  0.57189542  0.55977011  0.38134058  0.50802139  0.47916667
  0.47153537  0.3797519   0.46071429  0.49       ]
```

Model selection

There are a number of hyper parameters that can be adjusted to improve performance. It is often not a straightforward process, determining the effect of the various parameters, both individually and in combination with each other. Common things to try include getting more training examples, adding or removing features, adding polynomial features, and increasing or decreasing the regularization parameter. Given that we can spend a considerable amount of time collecting more data, or manipulating data in other ways, it is important that the time you spend is likely to result in a productive outcome. One of the most important ways to do this is using a process known as grid search.

Gridsearch

The `sklearn.grid_search.GridSearchCV` object is used to perform an exhaustive search on specified parameter values. This allows iteration through defined sets of parameters and the reporting of the result in the form of various metrics. The important parameters for `GridSearchCV` objects are an estimator and a parameter grid. The `param_grid` parameter is a dictionary, or list of dictionaries, with parameter names as keys and a list of parameter settings to try as values. This enables searching over any sequence of the estimators parameter values. Any of an estimator's adjustable parameters can be used with grid search. By default, grid search uses the `score()` function of the estimator to evaluate a parameter value. For classification, this is the accuracy, and as we have seen, this may not be the best measure. In this example, we set the scoring parameter of the `GridSearchCV` object to `f1`.

In the following code, we perform a search over a range of `C` values (the inverse regularization parameter), under both L1 and L2 regularization. We use the `metrics.classification_report` class to print out a detailed classification report:

```
from sklearn import datasets
from sklearn.cross_validation import train_test_split
from sklearn.grid_search import GridSearchCV
from sklearn.metrics import classification_report
from sklearn.linear_model import LogisticRegression as lr


X,y=datasets.make_blobs(n_samples=800,centers=2, random_state=0, cluster_std=4)
X_train, X_test, y_train, y_test = train_test_split(
    X, y, test_size=0.5, random_state=0)
tuned_parameters = [{'penalty': ['l1'],
                     'C': [0.01, 0.1, 1, 5]},
                    {'penalty': ['l2'], 'C': [0.01, 0.1, 1, 5]}]
scores = ['precision', 'recall','f1']
for score in scores:
    clf = GridSearchCV(lr(C=1), tuned_parameters, cv=5,
                       scoring='%s_weighted' % score)
    clf.fit(X_train, y_train)
    print("Best parameters on development set:")
    print()
    print(clf.best_params_)
    print("Grid scores on development set:")
    for params, mean_score, scores in clf.grid_scores_:
        print("%0.3f (+/-%0.03f) for %r"
              % (mean_score, scores.std() * 2, params))
    print("classification report:")
    y_true, y_pred = y_test, clf.predict(X_test)
    print(classification_report(y_true, y_pred))
```

We observe the following output:

```
Best parameters on development set:
{'penalty': 'l1', 'C': 0.1}
Grid scores on development set:
0.680 (+/-0.069) for {'penalty': 'l1', 'C': 0.01}
0.707 (+/-0.121) for {'penalty': 'l1', 'C': 0.1}
0.695 (+/-0.122) for {'penalty': 'l1', 'C': 1}
0.699 (+/-0.128) for {'penalty': 'l1', 'C': 5}
0.706 (+/-0.111) for {'penalty': 'l2', 'C': 0.01}
0.697 (+/-0.112) for {'penalty': 'l2', 'C': 0.1}
0.702 (+/-0.132) for {'penalty': 'l2', 'C': 1}
0.702 (+/-0.132) for {'penalty': 'l2', 'C': 5}
classification report:
             precision    recall   f1-score    support

          0       0.62      0.77       0.69        189
          1       0.73      0.58       0.65        211

avg / total       0.68      0.67       0.67        400
```

Grid search is probably the most used method of optimization hyper parameters, however, there are times when it may not be the best choice. The RandomizedSearchCV object implements a randomized search over possible parameters. It uses a dictionary similar to the GridSearchCV object, however, for each parameter, a distribution can be set, over which a random search of values will be made. If the dictionary contains a list of values, then these will be sampled uniformly. Additionally, the RandomizedSearchCV object also contains an n_iter parameter that is effectively a computational budget of the number of parameter settings sampled. It defaults to 10, and at high values, will generally give better results. However, this is at the expense of runtime.

There are alternatives to the *brute force* approach of the grid search, and these are provided in estimators such as LassoCV and ElasticNetCV. Here, the estimator itself optimizes its regularization parameter by fitting it along a regularization, *path*. This is usually more efficient than using a grid search.

Learning curves

An important way to understand how a model is performing is by using learning curves. Consider what happens to the training and test errors as we increase the number of samples. Consider a simple linear model. With few training samples, it is very easy for it to fit the parameters, the training error will be small. As the training set grows, it becomes harder to fit, and the average training error will likely grow. On the other hand, the cross validation error will likely decrease, at least at the beginning, as samples are added. With more samples to train on, the model will be better able to acclimatize to new samples. Consider a model with high bias, for example, a simple linear classifier with two parameters. This is just a straight line, so as we start adding training examples, the cross validation error will initially decrease. However, after a certain point, adding training examples will not reduce the error significantly simply because of the limitations of a straight line, it simply cannot fit nonlinear data. If we look at the training error, we see that, like earlier, it initially increases with more training samples, and at a certain point, it will approximately equal the cross validation error. Both the cross validation and train errors will be high in a high-bias example. What this shows is that if we know our learning algorithm has high bias, then just adding more training examples will be unlikely to improve the model significantly.

Now, consider a model with high variance, say with a large number of polynomial terms, and a small value for the regularization parameter. As we add more samples, the training error will increase slowly but remain relatively small. As more training samples are added the error on the cross validation set will decrease. This is an indication of over-fitting. The indicative characteristic of a model with high variance is a large difference between the training error and the test error. What this is showing is that increasing training examples will lower the cross validation error, and therefore, adding training samples is a likely way to improve a model with high variance.

In the following code, we use the learning curve object to plot the test error and the training error as we increase the sample size. This should give you an indication when a particular model is suffering from high bias or high variance. In this case, we are using a logistic regression model. We can see from the output of this code that the model may be suffering from bias, since both the training test errors are relatively high:

```
from sklearn.pipeline import Pipeline
from sklearn.learning_curve import learning_curve
import matplotlib.pyplot as plt
import numpy as np
from sklearn.preprocessing import StandardScaler
from sklearn.linear_model import LogisticRegression
```

```
from sklearn import cross_validation
from sklearn import datasets


X, y = datasets.make_classification(n_samples=2000,n_informative=2, n_
redundant=0,random_state=42)
Xtrain, Xtest, ytrain, ytest = cross_validation.train_test_split(X, y,
test_size=0.5, random_state=1)
pipe = Pipeline ([('sc' , StandardScaler()),('clf', LogisticRegression(
penalty = 'l2'))])
trainSizes, trainScores, testScores = learning_curve(estimator=pipe,
X=Xtrain, y= ytrain,train_sizes=np.linspace(0.1,1,10),cv=10, n_jobs=1)
trainMeanErr=1-np.mean(trainScores, axis=1)
testMeanErr=1-np.mean(testScores, axis=1)
plt.plot(trainSizes, trainMeanErr, color='red', marker='o', markersize=5,
label = 'training error')
plt.plot(trainSizes, testMeanErr, color='green', marker='s',
markersize=5, label = 'test error')
plt.grid()
plt.xlabel('Number of Training Samples')
plt.ylabel('Error')
plt.legend(loc=0)
plt.show()
```

Here is the output of the preceding code:

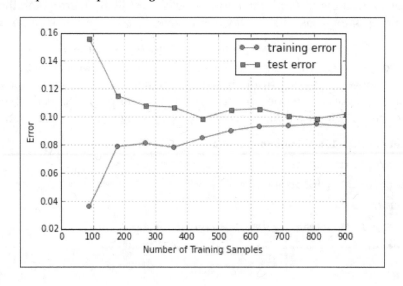

Real-world case studies

Now, we will move on to some real-world machine learning scenarios. First, we will build a recommender system, and then we will look into some integrated pest management systems in greenhouses.

Building a recommender system

Recommender systems are a type of information filtering, and there are two general approaches: **content-based filtering** and **collaborative filtering**. In content-based filtering, the system attempts to model a user's long term interests and select items based on this. On the other hand, collaborative filtering chooses items based on the correlation with items chosen by people with similar preferences. As you would expect, many systems use a hybrid of these two approaches.

Content-based filtering

Content-based filtering uses the content of items, which is represented as a set of descriptor terms, and matches them with a user profile. A user profile is constructed using the same terms extracted from items that the user has previously viewed. A typical online book store will extract key terms from texts to create a user profile and to make recommendations. This procedure of extracting these terms can be automated in many cases, although in situations where specific domain knowledge is required, these terms may need to be added manually. The manual addition of terms is particularly relevant when dealing with non-text based items. It is relatively easy to extract key terms from, say, a library of books, say by associating fender amplifiers with electric guitars. In many cases, this will involve a human creating these associations based on specific domain knowledge, say by associating fender amplifiers with electric guitars. Once this is constructed, we need to choose a learning algorithm that can learn a user profile and make appropriate recommendations. The two models that are most often used are the vector space model and the latent semantic indexing model. With the vector space model, we create a sparse vector representing a document where each distinct term in a document corresponds to a dimension of the vector. Weights are used to indicate whether a term appears in a document. When it does appear, it shows the weight of 1, and when it does not, it shows the weight of 0. Weights based on the number of times a word appears are also used.

The alternative model, latent semantic indexing, can improve the vector model in several ways. Consider the fact that the same concept is often described by many different words, that is, with synonyms. For example, we need to know that a computer monitor and computer screen are, for most purposes, the same thing. Also, consider that many words have more than one distinct meaning, for example, the word *mouse* can either be an animal or a computer interface. Semantic indexing incorporates this information by building a **term-document** matrix. Each entry represents the number of occurrences of a particular term in the document. There is one row for each of the terms in a set of documents, and there is one column for every document. Through a mathematical process known as single value decomposition this single matrix can be decomposed into three matrices representing documents and terms as vectors of factor values. Essentially this is a dimension reduction technique whereby we create single features that represent multiple words. A recommendation is made based on these derived features. This recommendation is based on semantic relationships within the document rather than simply matching on identical words. The disadvantages of this technique is that it is computationally expensive and may be slow to run. This can be a significant constraint for a recommender system that has to work in realtime.

Collaborative filtering

Collaborative filtering takes a different approach and is used in a variety of settings, particularly, in the context of social media, and there are a variety of ways to implement it. Most take a *neighborhood* approach. This is based on the idea that you are more likely to trust your friends' recommendations, or those with similar interests, rather than people you have less in common with.

In this approach, a weighted average of the recommendations of other people is used. The weights are determined by the correlation between individuals. That is, those with similar preferences will be weighted higher than those that are less similar. In a large system with many thousands of users, it becomes infeasible to calculate all the weights at runtime. Instead, the recommendations of a *neighborhood* are used. This neighborhood is selected either by using a certain weight threshold, or by selecting based on the highest correlation.

n the following code, we use a dictionary of users and their ratings of music albums. The geometric nature of this model is most apparent when we plot users' ratings of two albums. It is easy to see that the distance between users on the plot is a good indication of how similar their ratings are. The Euclidean distance measures how far apart users are, in terms of how closely their preferences match. We also need a way to take into account associations between two people, and for this we use the Pearson correlation index. Once we can compute the similarity between users, we rank them in order of similarity. From here, we can work out what albums could be recommended. This is done by multiplying the similarity score of each user by their ratings. This is then summed and divided by the similarity score, essentially calculating a weighted average based on the similarity score.

Another approach is to find the similarities between items. This is called **item-based collaborative filtering**; this in contrast with user-based collaborative filtering, which we used to calculate the similarity score. The item-based approach is to find similar items for each item. Once we have the similarities between all the albums, we can generate recommendations for a particular user.

Let's take a look at a sample code implementation:

```python
import pandas as pd
from scipy.stats import pearsonr
import matplotlib.pyplot as plt


userRatings={'Dave': {'Dark Side of Moon': 9.0,
  'Hard Road': 6.5,'Symphony 5': 8.0,'Blood Cells': 4.0},'Jen': {'Hard
Road': 7.0,'Symphony 5': 4.5,'Abbey Road':8.5,'Ziggy Stardust': 9,'Best
Of Miles':7},'Roy': {'Dark Side of Moon': 7.0,'Hard Road': 3.5,'Blood
Cells': 4,'Vitalogy': 6.0,'Ziggy Stardust': 8,'Legend': 7.0,'Abbey
Road': 4},'Rob': {'Mass in B minor': 10,'Symphony 5': 9.5,'Blood Cells':
3.5,'Ziggy Stardust': 8,'Black Star': 9.5,'Abbey Road': 7.5},'Sam':
{'Hard Road': 8.5,'Vitalogy': 5.0,'Legend': 8.0,'Ziggy Stardust':
9.5,'U2 Live': 7.5,'Legend': 9.0,'Abbey Road': 2},'Tom': {'Symphony 5':
4,'U2 Live': 7.5,'Vitalogy': 7.0,'Abbey Road': 4.5},'Kate': {'Horses':
8.0,'Symphony 5': 6.5,'Ziggy Stardust': 8.5,'Hard Road': 6.0,'Legend':
8.0,'Blood Cells': 9,'Abbey Road': 6}}


# Returns a distance-based similarity score for user1 and user2
def distance(prefs,user1,user2):
    # Get the list of shared_items
    si={}
```

```
        for item in prefs[user1]:
            if item in prefs[user2]:
                si[item]=1
        # if they have no ratings in common, return 0
        if len(si)==0: return 0
        # Add up the squares of all the differences
        sum_of_squares=sum([pow(prefs[user1][item]-prefs[user2][item],2)
        for item in prefs[user1] if item in prefs[user2]])
        return 1/(1+sum_of_squares)


def Matches(prefs,person,n=5,similarity=pearsonr):
    scores=[(similarity(prefs,person,other),other)
        for other in prefs if other!=person]
    scores.sort( )
    scores.reverse( )
    return scores[0:n]


def getRecommendations(prefs,person,similarity=pearsonr):
    totals={}
    simSums={}
    for other in prefs:
        if other==person: continue
        sim=similarity(prefs,person,other)
        if sim<=0: continue
        for item in prefs[other]:
            # only score albums not yet rated
            if item not in prefs[person] or prefs[person][item]==0:
                # Similarity * Score
                totals.setdefault(item,0)
                totals[item]+=prefs[other][item]*sim
                # Sum of similarities
                simSums.setdefault(item,0)
                simSums[item]+=sim
    # Create a normalized list
    rankings=[(total/simSums[item],item) for item,total in totals.items(
)]
    # Return a sorted list
    rankings.sort( )
```

```
    rankings.reverse( )
    return rankings


def transformPrefs(prefs):
    result={}
    for person in prefs:
        for item in prefs[person]:
            result.setdefault(item,{})
            # Flip item and person
            result[item][person]=prefs[person][item]
    return result


transformPrefs(userRatings)


def calculateSimilarItems(prefs,n=10):
    # Create a dictionary similar items
    result={}
    # Invert the preference matrix to be item-centric
    itemPrefs=transformPrefs(prefs)
    for item in itemPrefs:
#         if c%100==0: print("%d / %d" % (c,len(itemPrefs)))
        scores=Matches(itemPrefs,item,n=n,similarity=distance)
        result[item]=scores
    return result


def getRecommendedItems(prefs,itemMatch,user):
    userRatings=prefs[user]
    scores={}
    totalSim={}

    # Loop over items rated by this user
    for (item,rating) in userRatings.items( ):

        # Loop over items similar to this one
        for (similarity,item2) in itemMatch[item]:

            # Ignore if this user has already rated this item
            if item2 in userRatings: continue
```

```
            # Weighted sum of rating times similarity
            scores.setdefault(item2,0)
            scores[item2]+=similarity*rating

            # Sum of all the similarities
            totalSim.setdefault(item2,0)
            totalSim[item2]+=similarity

    # Divide each total score by total weighting to get an average
    rankings=[(score/totalSim[item],item) for item,score in scores.items(
)]

    # Return the rankings from highest to lowest
    rankings.sort()
    rankings.reverse()
    return rankings

itemsim=calculateSimilarItems(userRatings)

def plotDistance(album1, album2):
    data=[]
    for i in userRatings.keys():
        try:
            data.append((i,userRatings[i][album1], userRatings[i]
[album2]))
        except:
            pass
    df=pd.DataFrame(data=data, columns = ['user', album1, album2])
    plt.scatter(df[album1],df[album2])
    plt.xlabel(album1)
    plt.ylabel(album2)
    for i,t in enumerate(df.user):
        plt.annotate(t,(df[album1][i], df[album2][i]))
    plt.show()
    print(df)

plotDistance('Abbey Road', 'Ziggy Stardust')
print(getRecommendedItems(userRatings, itemsim,'Dave'))
```

You will observe the following output:

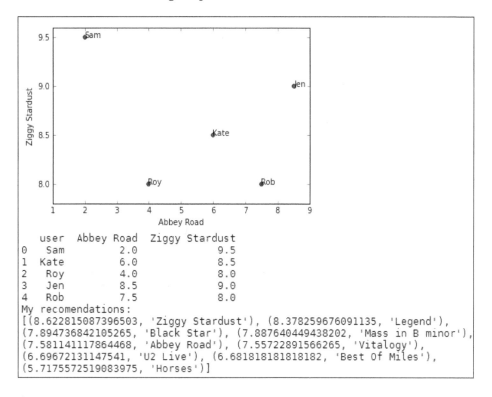

```
    user  Abbey Road  Ziggy Stardust
0   Sam          2.0             9.5
1  Kate          6.0             8.5
2   Roy          4.0             8.0
3   Jen          8.5             9.0
4   Rob          7.5             8.0
My recomendations:
[(8.622815087396503, 'Ziggy Stardust'), (8.378259676091135, 'Legend'),
(7.894736842105265, 'Black Star'), (7.887640449438202, 'Mass in B minor'),
(7.581141117864468, 'Abbey Road'), (7.55722891566265, 'Vitalogy'),
(6.69672131147541, 'U2 Live'), (6.681818181818182, 'Best Of Miles'),
(5.7175572519083975, 'Horses')]
```

Here we have plotted the user ratings of two albums, and based on this, we can see that the users **Kate** and **Rob** are relatively close, that is, their preferences with regard to these two albums are similar. On the other hand, the users **Rob** and **Sam** are far apart, indicating different preferences for these two albums. We also print out recommendations for the user **Dave** and the similarity score for each album recommended.

Since collaborative filtering is reliant on the ratings of other users, a problem arises when the number of documents becomes much larger than the number of ratings, so the number of items that a user has rated is a tiny proportion of all the items. There are a few different approaches to help you fix this. Ratings can be inferred from the type of items they browse for on the site. Another way is to supplement the ratings of users with content-based filtering in a hybrid approach.

Reviewing the case study

Some important aspects of this case study are as follows:

- It is part of a web application. It must run in realtime, and it relies on user interactivity.

- There are extensive practical and theoretical resources available. This is a well thought out problem and has several well defined solutions. We do not have to reinvent the wheel.

- This is largely a marketing project. It has a quantifiable metric of success in that of sale volumes based on recommendation.

- The cost of failure is relatively low. A small level of error is acceptable.

Insect detection in greenhouses

A growing population and increasing climate variability pose unique challenges for agriculture in the 21st century. The ability of controlled environments, such as greenhouses, to provide optimum growing conditions and maximize the efficient use of inputs, such as water and nutrients, will enable us to continue to feed growing populations in a changing global climate.

There are many food production systems that today are largely automated, and these can be quite sophisticated. Aquaculture systems can cycle nutrients and water between fish tanks and growing racks, in essence, creating a very simple ecology in an artificial environment. The nutrient content of the water is regulated, as are the temperature, moisture levels, humidity, and carbon dioxide levels. These features exist within very precise ranges to optimize for production.

The environmental conditions inside greenhouses can be very conducive to the rapid spread of disease and pests. Early detection and the detection of precursor symptoms, such as fungi or insect egg production, are essential to managing these diseases and pests. For environmental, food quality, and economic reasons, we want to only apply minimum targeted controls, since this mostly involves the application, a pesticide, or any other bio agent.

The goal here is to create an automated system that will detect the type and location of a disease or insect and subsequently choose, and ideally implement, a control. This is quite a large undertaking with a number of different components. Many of the technologies exist separately, but here we are combining them in a number of non-standard ways. The approach is largely experimental:

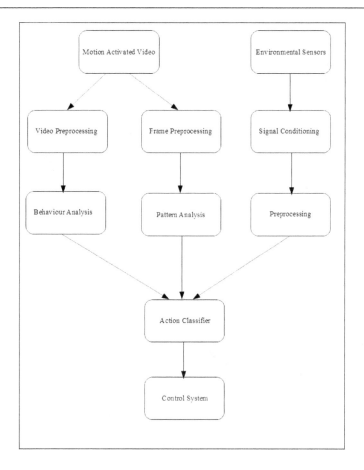

The usual method of detection has been direct human observation. This is a very time intensive task and requires some particular skills. It is also very error prone. Automating this would be of huge benefit in itself, as well as being an important starting point for creating an automated IPM system. One of the first tasks is to define a set of indicators for each of the targets. A natural approach would be to get an expert, or a panel of experts, to classify short video clips as either being pest free or infected with one or more target species. Next, a classifier is trained on these clips, and hopefully, it is able to obtain a prediction. This approach has been used in the past, for example, *Early Pest Detection in Greenhouses* (Martin, Moisan, 2004), in the detection of insect pests.

In a typical setup, video cameras are placed throughout the greenhouse to maximize the sampling area. For the early detection of pests, key plant organs such as the stems, leaf nodes, and other areas are targeted. Since video and image analysis can be computationally expensive, motion sensitive cameras that are intelligently programmed to begin recording when they detect insect movement can be used.

The changes in early outbreaks are quite subtle and can be indicated to be a combination of plant damage, discolorations, reduced growth, and the presence of insects or their eggs. This difficulty is compounded by the variable light conditions in greenhouses. A way of coping with these issues is to use a cognitive vision approach. This divides the problem into a number of sub-problems, each of which is context dependent. For example, the use a different model for when it is sunny, or based on the light conditions at different times of the day. The knowledge of this context can be built into the model at a preliminary, weak learning stage. This gives it an inbuilt heuristic to apply an appropriate learning algorithm in a given context.

An important requirement is that we distinguish between different insect species, and a way to do this is by capturing the dynamic components of insects, that is, their behavior. Many insects can be distinguished by their type of movement, for example, flying in tight circles, or stationary most of the time with short bursts of flight. Also, insects may have other behaviors, such as mating or laying eggs, that might be an important indicator of a control being required.

Monitoring can occur over a number of channels, most notably video and still photography, as well as using signals from other sensors such as infrared, temperature, and humidity sensors. All these inputs need to be time and location stamped so that they can be used meaningfully in a machine learning model.

Video processing first involves subtracting the background and isolating the moving components of the sequence. At the pixel-level, the lighting condition results in a variation of intensity, saturation, and inter-pixel contrast. At the image level, conditions such as shadows affect only a portion of the image, whereas backlighting affects the entire image.

In this example, we extract frames from the video recordings and process them in their own separate path in the system. As opposed to video processing, where we were interested in the sequence of frames over time in an effort to detect movement, here we are interested in single frames from several cameras, focused on the same location at the same time. This way, we can build up a three-dimensional model, and this can be useful, especially for tracking changes to biomass volume.

The final inputs for our machine learning model are environmental sensors. Standard control systems measure temperature, relative humidity, carbon dioxide levels, and light. In addition, hyper-spectral and multi-spectral sensors are capable of detecting frequencies outside the visible spectrum. The nature of these signals requires their own distinctive processing paths. As an example of how they might be used, consider that one of our targets is a fungus that we know exists in a narrow range of humidity and temperature. Supposing an ultraviolet sensor in a part of the greenhouse briefly detects the frequency range indicative of the fungi. Our model would register this, and if the humidity and temperature are in this range, then a control may be initiated. This control may be simply the opening of a vent or the switching on of a fan near the possible outbreak to locally cool the region to a temperature at which the fungi cannot survive.

Clearly, the most complex part of the system is the action controller. This really comprises of two elements: A multi label classifier outputting a binary vector representing the presence or not of the target pests and the action classifier itself which outputs a control strategy.

There are many different components and a number of distinct systems that are needed to detect the various pathogens and pests. The standard approach has been to create a separate learning model for each target. This multi-model approach works if we are instigating controls for each of these as separate, unrelated activities. However, many of the processes, such as the development and spread of disease and a sudden outbreak of insects, may be precipitated by a common cause.

Reviewing the case study

Some important aspects of this case study are as follows:

- It is largely a research project. It has a long timeline involving a large space of unknowns.

- It comprises a number of interrelated systems. Each one can be worked on separately, but at some point needs to be integrated back into the entire system.

- It requires significant domain knowledge.

Machine learning at a glance

The physical design process (involving humans, decisions, constraints, and the most potent of all: unpredictability) has parallels with the machine learning systems we are building. The decision boundary of a classifier, data constraints, and the uses of randomness to initialize or introduce diversity in models are just three connections we can make. The deeper question is how far can we take this analogy. If we are trying to build artificial intelligence, the question is, "Are we trying to replicate the process of human intelligence, or simply imitate its consequences, that is, make a reasonable decision?" This of course is ripe for vigorous philosophical discussion and, though interesting, is largely irrelevant to the present discussion. The important point, however, is that much can be learned from observing natural systems, such as the brain, and attempting to mimic their actions.

Real human decision making occurs in a wider context of complex brain action, and in the setting of a design process, the decisions we make are often group decisions. The analogy to an artificial neural net ensemble is irresistible. Like with an ensemble of learning candidates with mostly weak learners, the decisions made, over the lifespan of a project, will end up with a result far greater than any individual contribution. Importantly, an incorrect decision, analogous say to a poor split in a decision tree, is not wasted time since part of the role of weak learners is to rule out incorrect possibilities. In a complex machine learning project, it can be frustrating to realize that much of the work done does not directly lead to a successful result. The initial focus should be on providing convincing arguments that a positive result is possible.

The analogy between machine learning systems and the design process itself is, of course, over simplistic. There are many things in team dynamics that are not represented by a machine learning ensemble. For example, human decision making occurs in the rather illusive context of emotion, intuition, and a lifetime of experience. Also, team dynamics are often shaped by personnel ambition, subtle prejudices, and by relationships between team members. Importantly, managing a team must be integrated into the design process.

A machine learning project of any scale will require collaboration. The space is simply too large for any one person to be fully cognizant of all the different interrelated elements. Even the simple demonstration tasks outlined in this book would not be possible if it were not for the effort of many people developing the theory, writing the base algorithms, and collecting and organizing data.

Successfully orchestrating a major project within time and resource constraints requires significant skill, and these are not necessarily the skills of a software engineer or a data scientist. Obviously, we must define what success, in any given context, means. A theoretical research project either disproving or proving a particular theory with a degree of certainty, or a small degree of uncertainty, is considered a success. Understanding the constraints may give us realistic expectations, in other words, an achievable metric of success.

One of the most common and persistent constraints is that of insufficient, or inaccurate, data. The data collection methodology is such an important aspect, yet in many projects it is overlooked. The data collection process is interactive. It is impossible to interrogate any dynamic system without changing that system. Also, some components of a system are simply easier to observe than others, and therefore, may become inaccurate representations of wider unobserved, or unobservable, components. In many cases, what we know about a complex system is dwarfed by what we do not know. This uncertainty is embedded in the stochastic nature of physical reality, and it is the reason that we must resort to probabilities in any predictive task. Deciding what level of probability is acceptable for a given action, say to treat a potential patient based on the estimated probability of a disease, depends on the consequences of treating the disease or not, and this usually relies on humans, either the doctor or the patient, to make the final decision. There are many issues outside the domain that may influence such a decision.

Human problem solving, although sharing many similarities, is the fundamental difference from machine problem solving. It is dependent on so many things, not least of which is the emotional and physical state, that is, the chemical and electrical bath a nervous system is enveloped in. Human thought is not a deterministic process, and this is actually a good thing because it enables us to solve problems in novel ways. Creative problem solving involves the ability to link disparate ideas or concepts. Often, the inspiration for this comes from an entirely irrelevant event, the proverbial Newton's apple. The ability of the human brain to knit these often random events of every day experience into some sort of coherent, meaningful structure is the illusive ability we aspire to build into our machines.

Summary

There is no doubt that the hardest thing to do in machine learning is to apply it to unique, previously unsolved problems. We have experimented with numerous example models and used some of the most popular algorithms for machine learning. The challenge is now to apply this knowledge to important new problems that you care about. I hope this book has taken you some way as an introduction to the possibilities of machine learning with Python.

Index

C

calibration 158
Canopy
  reference link 37
categorical features 151
central moment 152
challenges, Big Data
  about 65
  data variety 66, 67
  data velocity 65, 66
  data volume 65
classification error 100
closed form solution 126
collaborative filtering approach 195, 196
computational complexity 96
conjunctively separable 94
content-based filtering approach 195
corpora 76
cost function
  about 136
  minimizing 136-139
cost function, logistic regression 122, 123
coverage space 94
Cumulative Density Function (CDF) 72

D

data
  about 64
  cleaning 82, 83
  distributions 68-72
  models 67, 68
  obtaining, from application programming
     interfaces 78, 79
  obtaining, from databases 73
  obtaining, from images 78
  obtaining, from natural language 76, 77
  obtaining, from Web 73, 75
  reference link 49
  visualizing 84-86
databases
  used, for solving issues 68
data models
  about 67
  constraints 68

operations 68
structure 68
decision boundary 121
deep architecture 146
descriptive models 105
design principles
  about 5, 6
  question, types 6
  right question, asking 7
  tasks 8
  unified modeling language (UML) 28
discretization 156, 157
distro 37
divisive 157
downhill simplex algorithm 53

E

ElasticNet 116
ensemble
  strategies 181, 182
  techniques 182, 183
  types 167
ensemble techniques
  about 167, 168
  averaging method 167
  boosting method 167
entering variable 14
equal frequency discretization 156
equal width discretization 156
extra trees 170-173
ExtraTreesClassifier class 170
ExtraTreesRegressor class 170

F

feature
  calibration 158-162
  discretization 156, 157
  normalization 157, 158
  transforming 154-156
  types 150
feature types
  categorical features 151
  ordinal features 151
  quantitative features 150

Fourier Transform 80
functions, for impurity measures
  Entropy 101
  Gini index 100

G

gene expression coefficients 149
global 111
gradient boosting 179, 180
gradient checking 145, 146

H

Hadoop 65
hamming distance 151
human interface 2-4
hyper parameter 111
hypothesis space 91

I

imputation 162
inductive logic programming 154
instance space 91
integrated pest management systems
    greenhouses
  about 202-205
  reviewing 205
internal disjunction 93
IPython console 36, 37
item-based collaborative filtering 197

J

Jupyter
  reference link 36, 37

K

kernel trick 26
k-fold cross validation 188
k nearest neighbors (K-NN)
  about 55
  KNeighborsClassifier 55
  RadiusNeighborsClassifier 55
kurtosis 153

L

L1 norm 127
lambda 126
Large Hadron Collider 66
Lasso 116
lasso regression 127
learning curves
  using 193, 194
least general generalization (LGG) 92
least squares
  about 110
  gradient descent 111-116
  normal equation 116-118
leaving variable 14
linear models 109
Linear Programming (LP) 13
local minimum 111
logical models
  about 90
  computational complexity 96, 97
  coverage space 94, 95
  generality ordering 91, 92
  Probably Approximately Correct (PAC)
    learning 96, 97
  version space 93, 94
logistic calibration 159
logistic function 119
logistic regression
  about 118-121
  cost function 122, 123
logistic units 131-135

M

machine learning
  about 206, 207
  activities 5
MapReduce 65
margin 182
mathematical operations, NumPy
  about 42
  polynomial functions 43
  vectors 42
Matlab 36
Matplotlib 37-48

Probably Approximately Correct (PAC)
  learning 96
Python
  used, for machine learning 36

Q

quantitative features 150

R

random forest 169, 170
real-world case studies
  about 195
  integrated pest management systems
    greenhouses 202
  recommender system, building 195
Receiver Operator Characteristic
  (ROC) 160
recommender system
  building 195
  collaborative filtering approach 196-201
  content-based filtering approach 195
  reviewing 202
recurrent neural networks (RNNs) 147
regularization 125-127
ridge regression 127
Rosenbrock function 53
rule models
  ordered list approach 103, 104
  purity 101-103
  set-based rule models 105-107

S

sample complexity 96
scikit-learn 54-61
SciPy
  about 51-54
  packages 51
  reference link 52
SciPy stack
  about 37
  installing 37
  reference link 37
segment 16

set-based rule models 105-107
SGDClassifier 115
SGDRegressor 115
shrinkage 58
sigmoid function 119
signals
  about 80, 81
  data, obtaining from sound 81
similarity function 26
skewness 152
stacked generalization 182
stacking 182
standardized features 162
statistics
  about 151-153
  central tendency 152
  dispersion 151
  shape 151
Stochastic gradient descent 115
stratified cross validation 189
streaming processing 66
structured features 154
subgroup discovery 105
subspace sampling 168, 169
sum of the squared error 110
Support Vector Machines (SVM) 26

T

task classification
  binary classification 9
  multiclass classification 9
tasks
  about 8
  classification 9
  clustering 10
  dimensionality reduction 10, 11
  errors 11
  features 23-28
  linear programming 13, 14
  models 15, 16
  optimization problems 12
  regression 9
term-document matrix 196
Thrip 85

tree models
  about 97-99
  purity 100

U

unified modeling language (UML)
  about 28
  activity diagrams 30
  class diagrams 29
  object diagrams 30
  state diagrams 31

V

variance 109
version space 94

W

weak learnability 174
Whitefly 85
WordNet
  reference link 3
world database 73

www.ingramcontent.com/pod-product-compliance
Lightning Source LLC
LaVergne TN
LVHW081340050326
832903LV00024B/1230